WHEN DO TEACHERS TEACH

DOAK S. CAMPBELL

Convention Press

NASHVILLE   TENNESSEE

Library of Congress Catalog Card Number: 58-10181

Printed in the United States of America
10. o 58 R.R.D.

ABOUT THE AUTHOR

DOAK S. CAMPBELL was born in Scott County, Arkansas on November 16, 1888. He received the B.A. degree from Ouachita College, Arkadelphia, Arkansas in 1911; the A.M. degree from George Peabody College for Teachers, Nashville, Tennessee, in 1928; and the Ph.D. degree from the same college in 1930. Three universities—Ouachita, Stetson, and Florida Southern—have conferred on him the LL.D. degree.

Dr. Campbell has been an outstanding leader in the educational field. He served as superintendent of the State High School at Columbus, Arkansas, 1911-14. He was state secretary of the Baptist Young People's Union and the Religious Education Association, 1914-16. He served Central College, Conway, Arkansas as vice-president, 1916-20, and as president, 1920-28. During the period 1928-41 he served on the faculty at George Peabody College for Teachers. In 1941 he became president of Florida State University, Tallahassee, Florida.

He has served in numerous key positions on educational committees. He was consultant on the President's Advisory Committee on Education, 1937-38. Since 1954 he has been on the board of trustees of Peabody College. He is a member of the Sunday School Board of the Southern Baptist Convention.

On May 28, 1913, Doak Campbell married Helen Gray Smith. She died in 1938. On February 5, 1941, he married Edna Simmons. He has two children: Doak Sheridan and Elizabeth Caroline.

Dr. Campbell is listed in *Who's Who in America* (1957). He has written several professional books in the educational field. WHEN DO TEACHERS TEACH has long been popular in the Sunday School Training Course.

FOREWORD

When Do Teachers Teach was first published in 1934 under the joint authorship of H. C. Trumbull and Doak S. Campbell. In that volume the essential message of Doctor Trumbull's widely used book, *Teaching and Teachers,* was presented in abridged form. The original message and language of Doctor Trumbull were preserved wherever possible. Although the book met a very favorable reception many demands came from Sunday school workers for the writer to produce a book under his own authorship that would preserve the message and the spirit of the earlier book and at the same time embrace the more recent developments in the theory and practice of teaching. This book comes in response to these demands.

This is a book on general teaching problems. It does not attempt to set forth specific suggestions for teaching in the several departments of the Sunday school. Those who desire such specific suggestions are referred to the books on teaching provided for the various departments.

In the effort to produce a book that would be in accord with the best thought in the science and art of teaching, many workers in the field of general education and religious education together with the best available literature on teaching have been brought under tribute. The workers and books thus contributing are too numerous for special mention. Dr. Homer L. Grice and Dr. P. E. Burroughs in particular have rendered service and contributed material without which the book in its present form would not have been possible. To Doctor Grice and Doctor Burroughs as well as all others who have made contribution grateful acknowledgment is made.

Doak S. Campbell

THE SUNDAY SCHOOL TRAINING COURSE

The Sunday School Training Course prepared by the Sunday School Department of the Baptist Sunday School Board is one of the major means of promoting Sunday school work. Its influence is limited only by its use.

The six sections of the course include studies in Bible, doctrines, evangelism, Sunday school leadership and administration, teaching, age group studies, and special studies. The range of the course is broad, for the field of Sunday school work is broad and requires comprehensive and specific training. Sixteen books are required for the completion of each diploma.

The study of the Training Course is not to be limited to the present Sunday school workers. Most churches need twice as many workers as are now enlisted. This need can be supplied by training additional workers now. Members of the Young People's and Adult classes and older Intermediates should be led to study these books, for thereby will their services be assured. Parents will find help as they study what the Sunday school is trying to do.

SPECIAL NOTE TO INSTRUCTOR

During your teaching of this book will you check with the Sunday school superintendent and see if an accurate record of training for the workers is kept. If not, please urge him to set up such a file with an associate superintendent of training in charge. Filing materials—cards, envelopes, or loose-leaf sheets—may be ordered at nominal cost from your nearest Baptist Book Store.

A. V. WASHBURN
Secretary, Sunday School
Department
Baptist Sunday School Board

SOME PROJECTED VISUAL MATERIALS

For Use in Teaching This Book

The filmstrips in the *Teacher Improvement Series* relate so closely to the material in this book that they may be used in their entirety as a basis for the discussion of all or a part of the chapters, as indicated. The suggestions in the manuals will help you to plan for effective use of the filmstrips.

Chapters 1-2   *The Christian Teacher*
Chapter   3   *Selecting Aims*
Chapter   5   *Choosing Methods*
Chapter   8   *Planning a Lesson*
Chapter   9   *Testing Results*

As an extra-session project you may have your training class members view the film, *Sword of the Spirit* (13 min.), and then discuss how it illustrates learning a skill through activities.

CONTENTS

I. Why Teachers Teach...................... 7

II. Teachers Should Know What Teaching Is.... 19

III. Teachers Should Know Their Learners....... 38

IV. Teachers Should Know What They Would Teach 51

V. Teachers Should Know How to Teach........ 60

VI. Teachers Should Secure and Use the Interest of Their Learners 72

VII. Teachers Should Provide Suitable Learning Activities 82

VIII. Teachers Should Plan Their Teaching........ 92

IX. Teachers Should Test Their Teaching........ 100

Directions for the Teaching and Study of This Book for Credit...................... 109

I

WHY TEACHERS TEACH

"Sunday school teacher" and "Bible" do not appear in the title or in any chapter heading of this book; but the book is nevertheless for Sunday school teachers. It is assumed throughout that they are teaching in order to help their pupils know the Bible, take the right attitudes toward it, appreciate it properly, and make use of it in becoming increasingly Christlike. It is also assumed that both teachers and pupils will use either the Uniform or the Graded Lessons along with their study of the Bible and the consideration of the practical problems of everyday Christian living, and that they will enrich their teaching with such other subject matter as they may need to secure the best spiritual results from attending Sunday school.

Whatever lack of emphasis there may seem to be on the Bible and its great teachings on such matters as sin, salvation, Christian service, the Saviourhood and Lordship of Jesus Christ, the work of the Holy Spirit, and so forth, is due to the limitations of space, the purpose of the book, and the further fact that there are several other companion books that deal specifically with these important subjects.

There is more or less general agreement among Christians that Sunday school teaching, taken as a whole, is not nearly so effective as it ought to be. Of the more than two million Sunday school teachers in the United States, far too many have an insufficient knowledge of the Bible, church and denominational history, Christian doctrines and missions, and other essential subject matter. They have too limited an understanding of what teaching really is and of its main purpose. They do not adequately know educational principles and the useful teaching methods. They have not learned pupil life well enough nor have they realized sufficiently how important it is to know every pupil as an individual in order to teach him effectively. These and other shortcomings help to explain why many pupils attend irregularly, take little interest, and get little out of Sunday school attendance.

All teachers need to consider frankly and prayerfully the results they are getting from their teaching, to face the statements of the preceding paragraph with reference to their own teaching, to decide what they must do if they are to reach more pupils and hold them and do more for them than they have been doing. This book is written to help teachers as they face these and other pressing teaching problems. From private study and from class discussions they should come to understand more clearly what real teaching is, what it is for, and how it must be done, if pupils are to be won to an intelligent and vital faith in Christ as both Saviour and Lord. It should assist teachers in giving their pupils a proper understanding of the great teachings of the Bible, and, by helpful guidance both within and without the classroom, in building what they learn into Christian character.

Because the book is brief, it has been necessary to limit the number of illustrations and to give less space to many important topics than they deserve. Persistent effort has been made to use simple and non-technical language, but when one writes of educational problems and methods as simply as he may, one must use language that requires close attention. The contents of this book should stimulate thought, provoke discussion, arouse interest, grip attention, and awaken such desires and purposes to teach better that further study of more comprehensive books will follow.

The world desperately needs the Christian message. Everybody ought to go to school to Christ, for he alone can meet all human needs. Through those who teach in the various teaching agencies of the churches, Christ must do much of his teaching. Surely those of us who teach for him and want him to teach through us will do our best to become the kind of teachers that we ought to be in character and personality, in knowledge of the Bible and other essential subject matter, in knowledge of pupil life, in knowledge of teaching principles and methods, and in teaching abilities and skills.

More than ninety-five out of every hundred children in the United States between the ages of six and thirteen, and more than one-half of those from fourteen to seventeen are enrolled in the public and private day schools of the country. They are studying under a vast host of teachers who are steadily improving in their abilities and skills and are alert to anything that will help them to do their work better. We who teach some of these same children and youth and their parents cannot afford to take our work lightly nor to use the teaching methods of horse-and-buggy days. In country, town, and city we must keep pace with progress. We must be skilled workmen and know what is going on about us and in the lives of our pupils. We must know how to take the ageless truths of the Christian religion and so interpret and apply them to present-day living that people, seeing their value, will appropriate them for the salvation and enrichment of life.

The definite question that all of us must face is this: Are we willing to give of our substance, our time, and our effort to learn more truly what Sunday school teaching is, and how better to do it so that we may labor more vitally and effectively for Christ in a loving and sympathetic ministry to those whom we are happy to call our pupils?

And now, we raise the question, Why do teachers teach?

Exacting are the demands made upon Sunday school teachers, demands upon heart, energy, time. The home and the public school have shifted to the church much of the task of Christian religious education. Thus the Sunday school has come to hold a primacy in Christian teaching. The Sunday school teacher must give time and effort to his teaching ministry, both on Sunday and during the week. To be successful he must increasingly pursue extended and continuous studies in preparation for his tasks.

Why, then, do Sunday school teachers teach? Our public school teachers receive annually nearly a billion dollars for their services, but our Sunday school teachers receive no pay for services which, if they were paid only one dollar a week, would amount to more than one hundred million dollars a year. One asks again, Why do teachers teach?

Dr. George H. Betts tells of a Leadership Training class whose members gave such answers as the following to the question, Why do *you* teach?*

"My pastor came and asked me and I did not like to refuse."

"My best friend was teaching a class and wanted me to take one."

"There was a class without any regular teacher and my conscience began to hurt me."

"I remember the poor teaching I had received as a child and wanted to give the children something better if I could."

"I have my own boy in the nursery and so I thought that in common fairness I should do something in return for this service."

"I like the church crowd and was glad when the superintendent asked me to teach a class."

"I think I can truthfully say that I teach for no reason except my interest in religion and the church."

All of these reasons are good. Some are better than others, but is not the last one the best—an interest in religion and the church, a love for Christ and his church, and a resolve, because of that love, to minister lovingly to others in an effort to serve their best interests?

Why do *you* teach? What *motives* impel you to teach? Why do all of us Sunday school teachers teach? Let us

Teaching Religion Today, pages 17, 18.

make answer, and then judge the correctness of our
answers in the light of the rest of this chapter.

I. Teaching Is a Fundamental Need

Teaching is a fundamental need of the teacher because
God has so made us that we grow in knowledge and
grace and power as we share our experiences with others.
What one of us does not recall the added joy of some
happy experience when we shared it with another? Who,
when beset with sorrow, has not found comfort and
strength by sharing it with a sympathetic soul? Who
having had a personal experience with Jesus Christ, does
not remember the added joy that came from leading some
one else to share that experience? A glorious experience
with the prophets of God, with the writers of the "good
news," with the heroic letters of Paul, with the marvelous
revelations to John—all these enrich us the more when
we share them with others whom we would direct in the
way of Christ.

Teaching is also a fundamental need of the learner.
Growth—physical, mental, spiritual—is a characteristic
of every living person. The process goes on continuously.
If this growth is to be wholesome and healthful, two
things are necessary—proper food and wise direction.
These are not generated from within; they must be supplied from without. If we are to "grow up in all things
into him, who is the head, even Christ" (Eph. 4:15 ASV),
we must receive wise guidance that will direct us toward
the things of Christ. The necessity for this guidance does
not cease when we reach spiritual maturity any more
than the need for material food ceases when we reach
physical maturity. The process of providing this means
of growth we call teaching.

II. Christ Commands Teaching

No doubt, the answer that satisfies many a Sunday
school teacher is, I teach because Christ commands it.
This is a sufficient answer with any Christian for his
conduct, provided, of course, he clearly understands the

command so that he can intelligently obey it. "To obey is better than sacrifice"; but God does not expect blind obedience. The reasonableness of his commands may be recognized, and compliance is always possible.

In so far as the individual capabilities and opportunities will permit, the sublime command of Christ to teach all nations, to baptize them, to teach them to observe all that he has commanded, is a command to every Christian everywhere. It necessitates a continuous process of teaching as long as life lasts. With it is linked a glorious promise, that of his comforting presence "even to the end of the world." "Teaching them to observe all things whatsoever I have commanded you" is a large order. When we take it seriously, we more fully appreciate the magnitude of the task of Christian teaching, for we are to guide people everywhere into a saving knowledge of Jesus Christ through an experience of his grace. When we lead them to accept Christ, we may think that our major task has been done; but this is only the beginning: "teaching them to observe" calls for a variety of important teaching activities beyond reckoning, as we shall presently see.

When Christ gave the command, he also interpreted it. What, then, does he want us to do? He tells us plainly and simply: he wants observance. Observance of the sacred ordinances of the church? Yes, that and much more. He wants us to teach the observance of all things whatsoever he has commanded. Attitudes, appreciations, habits, conduct, behavior—these are the things in which our Lord is interested for our sakes, and they should, therefore, be the objectives or aims of our teaching. Because no one ever attains perfection in the realization of these aims, our teaching must include all from the youngest to the oldest. Christian growth, unlike physical growth, is possible as long as life lasts. Even Paul, toward the close of his life, said, "I count not myself to have apprehended: but this one thing I do, forgetting those things which are behind, I press on toward the mark for the prize of the high calling of God in Christ Jesus."

Why do we teach then? In order that people "may grow up in all things into him who is the head, even Christ."

III. TEACHERS OUGHT, OWE IT, TO TEACH

The author of the Epistle to the Hebrews (5:12 ASV) says a significant word to believers: "When by reason of the time ye ought to be teachers. . . ." Ye "ought," ye owe it, to be teachers. Having been themselves taught, these people owed it to teach others. Having learned, they were under obligation to teach. Those who know Christ and his Holy Word "ought," owe it, to be teachers. Knowledge involves stewardship. Every living soul who knows God and his revealed word is solemnly bound to teach what he knows to others.

One who knows a remedy ought, owes it, to tell others about that remedy. One who knows a way of escape for his imperiled fellows is bound by every sacred obligation to reveal his secret to his suffering comrades. If a physician should discover a remedy for a dread disease and be healed by the remedy, and then should go on and leave the world in darkness as to his wonderful discovery, he would be execrated by all men. Even so, believers who have found in the Word the great secret of life are sacredly bound to teach others the glad tidings. Among the surest and best of all ways to meet this "ought," to discharge this obligation, is to teach in the Sunday school.

IV. TEACHERS ARE ASKED TO DO ONLY THAT WHICH ALL CHRISTIANS SHOULD DO

All of the essential things demanded of the teacher are equally demanded of believers as such. Is the teacher expected to live an exemplary Christian life and to support the church with his presence and prayers? Is he called to study the Scriptures and to give their message to others? Is he asked to give energy and time, even to make sacrifices, that he may be a spiritual guide to others? Is he to give his life and heart to personal com-

panionship and friendships with a view to helping and
guiding growing life? Yes; but all of these every be-
liever is called to do. We teach because, when we become
teachers, we have better opportunities to do what we
are already obligated to do.

V. The Skills Required of Teachers Are Helpful in All Walks of Life

Whether they will admit it or not, all people are to
some extent teachers. The preacher is a teacher as well
as a preacher. The physician tries to teach his patients
how to get well and keep well. The lawyer wins or loses
according to his ability to bring about the changes that
he desires in courts and juries. Commerce, industry,
business, all these, involve teaching-learning processes.
We succeed in so far as we get others to adopt our ideas
and ideals.

All of this is illustrated by those who have taught
what is set forth in this book. Frequently, they report
that merchants, clerks, agents, and men and women in
all kinds of business come to them and say: "This will
help me in my business. I see that the very things that
are required of a good teacher are needed by all who do
business with their fellows." Must a teacher know his
pupils or learners, know how to work with others and
lead them to see and feel as he himself sees and feels?
Must he love and respect others in order to influence and
guide them? All these and other similar things he must
do if he would teach successfully, but they are needed
also by all people in their social, political, and commercial dealings with others.

VI. Teachers Teach Because of What They Have to Share

The great truths of the Bible are the imperative and
urgent needs of all from earliest childhood until the end
of old age. Only a few needs that the Bible meets can
be stated here, but they are suggestive of many others
that might be listed.

Courage. The message of the Bible inspires faith and produces courage, courage to think right, to do right; courage to say No and Yes; courage to live and to die. During the depression years of the 1930's, strong men who should have had the courage to face adversity committed suicide in surprising numbers. If they had been taught and had really learned the vital truths set forth in the Holy Scriptures, they would have had an unfailing source of courage to meet life's trials. A business man who had suffered far more than many came to the writer in the midst of difficult days and, with a clear, courageous note said: "Through it all I have pillowed my head on this word, 'I had fainted, unless I had believed to see the goodness of Jehovah in the land of the living'" (Psalms 27:13 ASV). Literally, thousands of men and women, beset by trials and facing heavy odds, find in the message of the holy Scriptures the courage that they need.

Consolation. Sorrow is man's common lot. Sooner or later darkness gathers about every home, and shadows fall on every heart. The message of the Bible, planted in the fertile soil of childhood, comes with solace and soothing in later years of trial. Who would not be a teacher and plant this wonderful seed which ever after will bear the fruit of comfort and consolation?

Confidence. Fear is the bane of life. Beginning early, vague, haunting fears disturb and distress us, even down to the drawing of the last fleeting breath. Nature grows violent; pestilence stalks abroad; storms devastate and destroy. Primitive men saw in all these the wrath of the gods and trembled with vague, disturbing fears. Science has done much to dispel these fears, but, even so, fear still abides and lays heavy trial on human hearts. As we walk the streets or ride the highways, we see fear in all too many faces. He is indeed a public benefactor who plants in human hearts the gentle, persuasive words of Jesus, "Come unto me, all ye that labor and are heavy laden, and I will give you rest" (Matt. 11:28 ASV).

Enriched Personality. Under the message and light of
the Old Testament Scriptures and the companionship and
teaching of Jesus, a group of Galilean peasants were
transformed into a company of heroic prophets and apos-
tles; for example, Simon the unstable became Peter the
rock. Such transformations have been wrought in all the
ages since. All about us are twiceborn men, remade
and renewed by divine grace. Personalities are enriched and men are glorified when they learn, believe,
receive and obey the revealed word of God.

VII. TEACHERS TEACH BECAUSE GOD IS A TEACHING GOD

In a peculiar sense the teacher walks in God's ways.
He who teaches the Way of Life as it is revealed in the
Bible must needs think God's thoughts after him. That
God is a teaching God may be seen in the fact that nature,
whose basal laws and practices reflect in some measure
his wisdom and goodness, magnifies the teaching-learning processes. Mother Nature, some one has well said,
is a real teacher, for by her rewards and penalties and
her unchanging law she ever helps men to learn.

That he is a teaching God is even more clearly seen
in the fact that his Son, who was "the brightness of his
glory and the express image of his person," came to the
earth as a teacher. Through a teaching ministry Jesus
revealed the Father; through teaching-learning processes
he still wins men to salvation and service. He ordained
that through teaching ministries the good news of life
and salvation should be carried to all the world: "Go
ye therefore, and make disciples [learners] of all the nations . . . teaching them to observe all things whatsoever
I commanded you: and lo, I am with you always, even
unto the end of the world" (Matt. 28:19-20).

TEACHING SUGGESTIONS

Questions for Study and Review

1. Why do you teach in the Sunday school? Is this a sufficient reason?
2. What are some typical answers given by Sunday school teachers?
3. In what respect is teaching a fundamental human need of the teacher? Of the learner?
4. What underlies Jesus' command to teach? What elements are involved in it?
5. Why do we "owe it" to teach?
6. What obligations does the teacher have that are not obligations of all Christians?
7. Compare the requirements for teaching with those of commercial or business relations.
8. What essential things in the Christian message impel us to teach?
9. In what respects is our God a teaching God?
10. In what sense are all Christians teachers?

Topical Outline

WHAT MOTIVES IMPEL TEACHERS TO TEACH

I. TEACHING A FUNDAMENTAL HUMAN NEED
   1. Of the teacher
   2. Of the learner

II. CHRIST COMMANDS TEACHING

III. WE TEACH BECAUSE WE "OWE" TO TEACH

IV. TEACHERS ARE ASKED TO DO ONLY THE THINGS WHICH ALL BELIEVERS SHOULD DO
   1. Live an exemplary Christian life
   2. Study the Scriptures and carry their message to others
   3. Give life and heart to service

V. THE GRACES ACQUIRED IN TEACHING CONTRIBUTE TO USEFULNESS AND SUCCESS IN ALL WALKS OF LIFE

VI. BECAUSE OF WHAT WE HAVE TO SHARE
The Truth of the Holy Scriptures
1. Inspires courage
2. Gives consolation
3. Engenders confidence
4. Develops enriched personality

VII. BECAUSE OUR GOD IS A TEACHING GOD
1. Revealed in nature
2. Revealed in his Son

II

TEACHERS SHOULD KNOW WHAT TEACHING IS

When do teachers really teach? How can they know what real teaching is; when that which is called teaching is actually teaching? This chapter is an effort to answer these questions.

Much confusion exists about what constitutes teaching. Many who profess to teach seem never to ask themselves if they are really teaching. Others, having discovered that they are not really teaching, experience difficulty in finding out wherein they are failing. Much time and effort are consumed in Sunday schools under the name of teaching that cannot rightly be so named. Many who have been chosen to teach do not even know what teaching actually is and cannot therefore know that they are not really teachers. They are teachers according to the records, but that does not make them teachers. Until they know when teachers really teach, and what teaching actually is, they cannot know whether they are merely teachers by the record or teachers in fact. There is a difference between filling a teacher's place and holding it.

I. NEGATIVE APPROACH

That we may understand what teaching is, it is helpful to consider first what it is not, and thereby clear up possible misconceptions.

1. *Telling Is Not Teaching*. Many Sunday school teachers seem to think that telling is teaching. It is an important phase, for, if teachers could not tell, they would be seriously handicapped in teaching, and their pupils would be similarly handicapped in learning. Telling in and of itself, however, is not and cannot be teach-

ing. Unless a person realizes this he is not prepared to teach. Suppose a teacher, with his head down so that the movement of his lips cannot be seen, tells a deaf pupil a truth! Is that teaching? Suppose, instead, that the pupil hears, but does not pay attention or understand the words which the teacher tells him. Is that teaching? Even if a person learns a part of what he is told, but does not learn it all, he is not fully taught, for he is taught no more than he learns. Telling a child the books of the Bible, the Golden Rule, or any biblical truth is not teaching him. One could easily learn to teach if telling were teaching.

Truth must be learned, and only the learner can learn it. Facts, information, and ideas are the materials of learning. Even when a learner gathers facts, gets information and lays hold of ideas, he will find them of little or no value until he can use them; then he will really learn them. Telling a person *how,* does not necessarily mean that he will *know* how. If it did, how quickly and easily everybody could learn to drive an automobile, play the piano, paint a picture, practice law, be a teacher or preacher or physician. What a boon it would be to drowning people if one could stand on the bank and tell them how to swim; and how easily it would be to rescue them! No, telling is not teaching; it may help, but much more is necessary.

2. *Hearing a Recitation Is Not Teaching.* Again, many Sunday school teachers seem to think that "hearing a lesson" or letting the pupils recite is teaching. Reciting by the pupil, like telling by the teacher, is an important phase of teaching. It may help the pupil to learn, but reciting has its limitations. Professor John S. Hart says truly: "A pupil recites lessons when he repeats something previously learned. A pupil is taught when he learns with the help of the teacher something not known before. The two things often, indeed, go together, but they are in themselves essentially distinct."

Recitation by pupils of any age is of relatively little value, for they may not know the meaning of the words they use or they may give them the wrong meaning. For them to recite the words under these conditions may mean that they have merely learned the words, and such reciting cannot be a proof to the teacher that the pupil has really learned. A child's answer to the first question of the Westminster Catechism was, "Manschefand is to glorify God and enjoy him forever." What that strange word meant, she did not know until years later. Reciting it to her teacher would have been proof, if the teacher had understood her, that she had not learned the answer to that first question. Memorizing words and being able to state ideas is no more learning truth than buying books is securing knowledge. A man might fill a library with books and still be ignorant of what is in them and of the values that they contain. In like manner, one may use words and state ideas and be ignorant of their meaning and value.

It cannot be said too often nor emphasized too much that the purpose of real teaching is to help learners acquire fruitful knowledge and develop such attitudes and build up such appreciations that they will use the knowledge in forming ideals, making resolutions (purposing), and acquiring skills for useful, happy living. Telling by the teacher and reciting by the pupil have their places in teaching, but how tragic it is if the teacher thinks that these constitute teaching!

II. POSITIVE APPROACH

It is not enough to show what teaching is not; it must also be shown what teaching actually is. Unfortunately, the dictionaries give us little help, since the definitions vary and are often vague and unsatisfactory. Even books on teaching sometimes fail to give clearly the scope and meaning of teaching. Authors and teachers frequently assume that the meaning of the word is well known, and then themselves leave some doubt as to just what it means.

Originally, "learn" was used in the sense of both teaching and learning: a person could learn by himself, or he could learn another; that is, help another to learn. The latter meaning appears in the words of the queen to her physician in Shakespeare's *Cymbeline:*

> Have I not been
> Thy pupil long? Hast thou not learned me how
> To make perfumes? distill? preserve?

Later, the distinction between the two meanings of the word was indicated by using "teaching" for what the teacher does, and "learning" for what the pupil does. "Teaching" is therefore that part of the teaching-learning process by which the teacher instructs, inspires, and guides the pupil in both making a truth his own and using it to achieve his purposes; and "learning" is that part of the same twofold process by which the learner makes the truth his own and uses it. There can be no teacher if there is no learner. There may be a learner where there is no teacher, for the learner may teach himself. In fact, that is the purpose of creative teaching— the teacher makes himself less and less essential to the learner as the learner increasingly learns how to teach himself or be his own teacher.

III. Phases of Teaching

A study of what is said in the following paragraphs may help us to get a better idea of what teaching is.

1. *Teaching Is Helping Another to Learn.* To learn, one must study, think, reason, imagine, feel, listen, talk, discuss, read, write, draw, and so forth. "Activities" is the word used to describe these various things that one does in order to learn. Note that some of the activities are mental, some emotional, some physical. To learn, a pupil must engage in activities, but what activities? How can he know what activities? Frequently, he does not know. That is why he needs a teacher—one who will select the kind of activities in which the learner may engage so that the desired learning will result, get him

to accept them as his own, and then guide him while *Field Trips*
he is engaging in them. Educationally speaking, then,
an activity is what a pupil does in order to learn something. It has a purpose back of it, and its nature is determined by what the pupil wants to learn. Different
types of learning call for different kinds of activities.

However, it is not enough for the teacher to plan
learning activities and get the pupils to accept them and
engage in them; that will not of itself guarantee the
desired learning. While they engage in the activities,
the pupils may have the wrong kind of experiences,
experiences which will keep them from learning what the
teacher wants them to learn. For example, a teacher
wants his pupils to learn what reverence is and to act
reverently. He plans for some activities to achieve his
aims; the pupils accept them and engage in them; but
during the activities they have some experiences that
result in their being less instead of more reverent. The
activities led to experiences, but they were not the type
of experiences that the teacher desired. It may be that
the teacher did not know how to guide the activities so
as to secure the desired meaningful experiences.

If a teacher would help his pupils learn, he must not
only plan the proper activities for them to accept and
engage in; he must also direct the activities in such a
way that the pupils will have the experiences that are
necessary in order that the desired learning will result.
We sometimes say that experience is the best teacher.
As a matter of fact, it is the only teacher, for "experience
includes both what one does on one hand, and on the
other hand what he undergoes." Often our best learning
experiences are vicarious; that is, we read of the experiences of another in a book, or see them portrayed in
the motion picture, or listen to them as they are read or
related by another. We enter into them as if they
were our own, identify ourselves with the hero or heroine
or some other character that appeals to us, and, for the
time being, cease to be ourselves. As a result we may
have many meaningful experiences in a very brief time.

All of this means that when we want our pupils to learn the facts about a biblical character, or to understand and believe a biblical doctrine, or to appreciate a biblical story, we must think of various learning activities and select those which in our judgment are most suitable and useful. Next, we must secure the co-operation of our pupils so that they will engage in these activities. Then, we must guide them in the activities so that they will have the very experiences which will result in the desired learning.

Frequently, this "helping another to learn" is stated as "causing another to know." "Helping" is the more desirable word, but "causing" is all right if we properly interpret and define it. "Helping" suggests personal relationship, a vital process, the co-operation of two in a united effort; it implies that both are necessary in accomplishing a purpose. In teaching, the teacher helps the pupil to learn what he could not learn, or learn so successfully, by himself. "Causing" suggests non-personal relationships, mechanical forces, acting and being acted upon, cause and effect. If we say that a teacher causes a pupil to know, we mean that the teacher initiates, makes plans, stimulates, stirs up, acts upon the pupil in such a way that his responses result in his acquiring fruitful knowledge, that which takes hold upon life and makes it different. As in the physical world every effect must have an adequate cause, so in the teaching world every effect (what the pupil comes to know) must have an adequate cause (what the teacher does to and for and with the pupil to assure his coming to know). Teaching by the teacher and learning by the pupil are therefore inseparable; they are two phases of one process.

2. *Teaching Is the Communication of Truth from Person to Person.* This well-known definition of preaching by Phillips Brooks is also a good definition of teaching. "Communication" is hardly the word to use, however, since it seems to suggest that truth can be literally passed from one mind to another. Instead, the teacher instructs,

inspires, and guides the learner as he tries to make the truth his very own.

3. *Teaching Is Guiding Growing Life.* A beautiful garden lies out in full view of the writer's window. In it are many varieties of unusually beautiful flowers and plants that the gardner loves. With ceaseless and self-forgetting care he feeds and protects the growing life. Like him, the teacher also protects and guides growing life.

To summarize, Sunday school teaching consists of those activities, planned by the teacher but accepted and engaged in by the pupils, out of which arise the meaningful experiences that enable the pupils to acquire fruitful knowledge, lay hold of truth and make it their own, and build it into life in such a manner that they become increasingly Christlike in thought and word and motive and deed—at home, in the church and the community, in business, in social life, in leisure activities, and as citizens—wherever they are, all of the time.

IV. TEACHING IN THE LIGHT OF ITS AIMS

As stated at the outset, the object of our teaching is set forth in the words of Jesus—"to observe all things whatsoever I have commanded you." To accomplish this complicated task involves a variety of activities both on the part of the teacher and the learner. These activities are frequently designated as types of teaching, whereas, they are in fact different aspects of the teaching-learning process.

1. *Teaching Is of Three Kinds: Factual, Ideational, and Creative*

First, there is what may be called "factual teaching." This involves the direction of learners in acquiring words, statements, facts. The factual aspect of teaching is important mainly because it furnishes the learner with the materials that he needs for achieving his purposes—further learning. With adults teaching may deal largely with facts to be learned because, as a result of previous experiences, they are interested in learning facts as facts. With younger pupils also many words, facts and statements are essential to the learning of other things that affect character and life. The Sunday school teacher must provide factual instruction, such as is found in history, biography, geography, and biblical antiquities in general, but he should think of it primarily as the basis of further and more vital teaching.

Second, there is what is frequently termed "ideational teaching." There are times when the teacher needs to give special emphasis to developing ideas or understandings. He attempts to teach an idea; for example, the idea of honesty. What is honesty? Why be honest? What are the rewards of honesty? The teacher may thus present honesty as an idea. He may also lead his pupils to accept honesty as an ideal, but the vital question remains, Will the pupils really know what honesty is and will they behave honestly? Presenting an idea is an important aspect of teaching, but its limitations should be recognized.

Third, there is what is generally called "creative teaching." It is the kind of teaching which helps the individual to acquire new values for himself, values which in turn lead to new incentives and the development of still other values. Sunday school teachers are to teach not religion merely, but the Christian religion, a religion that not only induces experience but is experience. If our teaching of the Christian religion does not make any difference in the lives of our pupils, the trouble must lie either with religion or the teaching of it. We can easily locate the trouble. Learning is change, and if there is no change, there is no learning; and if no learning, no teaching. The trouble is with the teaching, not with the Christian religion.

2. Aims or Objectives in Teaching

Why do we teach? What is our goal or purpose, our aim or objective? What changes do we want to bring about in the lives of those whom we teach? What do we want to help them become? Do we want them merely to master facts, gain information, secure biblical knowledge? Shall we stop with helping them to acquire ideas? How may we teach creatively so that increasingly, without a teacher's help, they may come not only *to know*, but also *to do*, the will of God?

What is an aim? Briefly stated, it is an end in view that serves the teacher as a constant guide as he directs the growth of his learners. Aims become effective in directing the teaching when the purposes of the learner are brought to coincide with the aims of the teacher. When stated too generally they are not effective. One cannot teach "in general." It is necessary, therefore, to state aims or objectives somewhat specifically. More and more the aims or objectives of teaching are being stated as helping pupils to acquire: (1) fruitful knowledge and beliefs; (2) desirable attitudes and loyalties; (3) worthy interests, appreciations and ideals; and (4) necessary abilities and skills.

We can separate these objectives in thought, but not in fact; they are interrelated and interacting. Knowledge affects attitudes; knowledge and attitudes largely control interests and appreciations; and knowledge, attitudes and interests express themselves in abilities and skills. These objectives, to whatever extent they are achieved, help the pupil to acquire an enriched personality and to build a more worthy Christian character.

(1) *Knowledge and Beliefs*

A fact is something that is, or is done, or happens. When a person can properly interpret the significance of a fact (show its relation to other facts), when he can use facts to discover principles, to understand truth, and to interpret correctly what is going on about him, he has knowledge. We often think of knowledge as information, as the possession of truth, as practical understanding. It varies in value. Some knowledge is of much, and some of little, worth. Some has much value to one person, but little to another, for it depends upon the use to which one can put it.

There is far more knowledge than any one can master. Common sense, therefore, suggests selection. We want to acquire that knowledge which will be most useful to us; that is, most fruitful. Since we are always pressed for time, we must select what knowledge we will try to acquire. Much valuable knowledge we must forego in order that we may secure what is still more valuable. We must keep this in mind with reference to biblical knowledge, for some biblical facts and information are of far more value than others, some teachings or doctrines are more significant and vital than others. For example, that pastor was a poor judge of knowledge who required everybody in his Sunday school to spend three months—thirteen Sundays—studying the location of the Twelve Tribes in the Promised Land.

The first step in building character or developing personality is to help learners acquire knowledge and beliefs. They should be like Timothy to whom Paul wrote, "From a child thou hast known the holy scriptures." Knowledge comes and beliefs develop as pupils learn. From good teaching they will in due time "come in the unity of the faith, and of the knowledge of the Son of God, unto a perfect man, unto the measure of the stature of the fulness of Christ."

Sunday school teaching, then, should lead to fruitful knowledge and beliefs; to knowledge where knowledge is possible, and to beliefs where one cannot really know. One can know, for example, that Jesus lived in Palestine during the first century, whereas he must believe that he was none other than the Christ of God, long promised through the prophets. One vital test of teaching must lie in the knowledge and beliefs that the learners gain. A boy is committed to your care and teaching for one year. At the end of the year one test of your teaching must be what he knows and believes as a result of your teaching. A pertinent question for every teacher to ask himself after every lesson is, What useful knowledge have my pupils acquired because of my teaching this week?

(2) *Attitudes and Loyalties*

It is not enough to help learners acquire fruitful knowledge and beliefs; we must help them to use their knowledge and beliefs in acquiring desirable attitudes and loyalties.

Attitudes. An attitude is "the state of mind of the individual towards a value." Attitudes include our dispositions, prejudices (prejudgments), and mental habits. They reveal what we will do. They reveal our past by showing what we have done and thought. They are our past experiences summed up in our present sets of mind and predispositions which influence our conduct in present and new situations. They are mental habits to which feeling is attached; no feeling or emotion, no attitude. Rooted in the past, they act in the present. They are revealed in the opinions which we have formed and the evaluations which we have made in the light of our traditions and experiences. They are largely the results of our environment. David Seabury says:

"An attitude is like a key; a wrong attitude closes a door, and a right attitude opens it. We want to get hold of those attitudes which will release our inner power; get hold of our drives that often come out in negative activities."

One's attitude towards any specific subject (truth, doctrine, deed) is the sum total of his inclinations towards it and feelings about it, his prejudices or bias, his preconceived ideas, notions, and fears, with reference to that subject. For example, his attitude towards prohibition is made up of all that he feels about the liquor traffic. One's attitudes toward oneself, toward others, toward one's church, toward Christ, are determined by how the individual feels towards himself and them, the experiences he has had himself and with them. Attitudes are, therefore, personal and subjective, and are revealers of how one will behave with reference to any given subject.

Attitudes may be right or wrong, desirable or undesirable. Some need to be eliminated, others improved, still others to be added. Pupils need guidance in experiences which will enable them to acquire desirable, and overcome undesirable attitudes. Every week, we should plan how to use lesson material and teaching situations for changing attitudes. This means, of course, that we must know what attitudes each pupil has, which need changing, which need re-enforcing, and what new ones he ought to acquire. Frequently it is difficult to eliminate a bad attitude—a prejudice, for example. Helping pupils to change or acquire attitudes is a slower and more difficult task, and requires more patience and skill, than helping them to acquire knowledge.

Loyalties. Attitudes are inseparable from loyalties; in fact, they largely determine loyalties. Loyalty suggests devotion to a person, a cause, a truth. It involves fidelity, allegiance and love; it suggests action (attack or defense), and secures stedfastness of purpose. It may lead to the giving of life itself for a person, a cause or a belief. Loyalty does not itself guarantee right motives and good character. One may misplace one's loyalties; for example, one may be loyal to a wrong cause or to unworthy people. One aim in teaching should be to help learners develop the right kind of loyalties—loyalty to Christ and the Christian way of living, loyalty to family, community, state, and nation, loyalty to great causes and noble ideals. Loyalties depend on attitudes and are partly revealed in one's appreciations or sense of values. They also depend upon knowledge, and they lead to conduct or behavior.

(3) *Interests, Appreciations, and Ideals*

Knowledge and beliefs underlie attitudes and loyalties, and these in turn underlie interests, appreciations, and ideals.

Interests. Interests control our activities and therefore our attention. They affect our feelings, shape our desires, and give meaning to our experiences. Our needs, real or supposed, determine our interests. We may misjudge our needs and therefore develop interests that do not really meet our needs. Interests may be worthy or unworthy, and they vary in intensity and persistence. Some interests may largely dominate us, and others concern us but little. One trouble with many Christians is that their interests are often unworthy and are a hindrance to the development of a Christlike character. It should be the aim of teachers to help pupils both to acquire worthy interests and to deepen those they already have. To do this they must think of ways by which they may help their pupils to use their biblical and other information in acquiring and developing worthy interests. These ways must include activities outside as well as inside the classroom.

Appreciations. Appreciation involves the ability to assign a value. We cannot appreciate what has no value to us or what we do not like or what we hate. We do appreciate what we admire, love, reverence, respond to joyfully. Appreciations have to do with values that are social, intellectual, esthetic, moral, and spiritual. They are satisfying emotional responses to things, persons, institutions, causes, and so forth.

If our valuations are wrong or unworthy, so will our appreciations be, and our enjoyment will come from that which is unworthy or less worthy. One may appreciate jazz rather than classical music; poor pictures rather than great Christian paintings; doggerel rather than poetry; cheap fiction rather than great novels; a demagogue rather than a statesman; a desperado rather than a Christian gentleman; war rather than peace.

As Sunday school teachers we must include among our aims that of helping our pupils to acquire worthy appreciations, especially in the realm of the religious and the spiritual. We want to help them not only to learn the facts and truths of the Bible; we also want to help them take and develop the right attitudes towards them, acquire the proper appreciations for them, manifest an abiding interest in them, and, as we shall presently see, build the right ideals upon them, and develop abilties and skills in using the teachings of the Bible in living a fruitful Christian life. We must plan to help our pupils increasingly to appreciate, not only the Bible but also the church, all Christian institutions and groups, and the Christian way of living. The importance of including appreciations in our objectives is all the more evident if we realize that an individual's appreciations largely control him in choosing his companions, determining his interests, and giving direction to his activities.

Ideals. Attitudes are rooted in the past, but act in the present. Appreciations and interests are concerned with the present. Ideals look to the future, but govern the activities of the present. Ideals are projected achievements accompanied by desire and purpose. They are contemplated experiences, goals possible to reach; they are worth what it may cost to reach them. An ideal may be no more than a trait or characteristic that is the object of desire and purpose, as courage to meet a situation; or it may be general in nature. One's ideals consist of all that one does not have, but values and purposes to get. They give direction and meaning to effort. One may lose an ideal. It may cease to have enough value for him to make him want to strive for it, or he may decide that it is not possible to attain it. One may persistently strive for a long time to make the ideal real and not succeed because he may not know how to attain it or may lack sufficient skill even if he knows how, or he may waste or poorly direct his efforts.

One's ideals may be low, unworthy, immoral; for example, one may want to excel in display, to be a successful bandit, or to get even with an enemy. It is not enough to have ideals, for every one has them; they must be the right kind. Worthy ideals are dependent upon fruitful knowledge and the right kind of attitudes, appreciations, and interests. Surely, one of our main duties and privileges is to assist our pupils in both forming and achieving worthy ideals. But what are worthy ideals? And what must we do to help our pupils achieve them? We must be able to define worthy ideals, and know what ideals our pupils have, what they need to purify, and what to form. We should include them in our objectives and week by week plan to use the lesson material and the class activities to help our pupils achieve their old ideals and form new ones.

(4) Abilities and Skills

To achieve our aims we lead our pupils into activities of various kinds—mental and physical. These activities result in learning products or outcomes, that we call "abilities." The function of abilities is to control and direct future conduct. If as the result of teaching, a pupil learns, for example, that multiplication is a short method of addition, his new knowledge is an "ability," and its function thereafter will be to control his conduct when he adds: instead of writing 25 down twenty-five times and adding to get the result, he will multiply 25 by 25 and save both time and paper.

Abilities are acquired, and they can be improved. Their proper use leads to useful habits and valuable skills, which tend to become automatic. We do many things without thinking that formerly required much thought and time and effort, and were even then poorly done. Abilities are acquired in the realm of the moral and spiritual as they are elsewhere. Religious habits are developed in the same way as are other habits. Skills in Christian living are developed in much the same way as other skills are developed. Abilities, habits, skills— these are vital among the objectives of our teaching. Knowledge is of but little or of no value unless it is put to use; if not used, it has no more value to its possessor than Robinson Crusoe's gold had for him when he was alone on his island. Attitudes, appreciations, interests, ideals—all of these are significant to the extent that they issue in fruitful thinking and doing, and make people more able to live worthily and happily.

Every week we should plan to help our pupils to acquire the fruitful knowledge that inheres in the lesson and related material, but we should not stop there as we so often do; we should also plan to help them to put this knowledge to increasingly effective use in building habits and developing skills for the richest and most fruitful Christian living.

If we are to have worthy objectives, we must know our pupils and their needs. If we are to achieve our objectives, we must know our subject matter and how to teach: how to plan a lesson, what methods to use and how to use them, how to arouse and use interest, how to guide activities, and what activities to select.

Truly, teaching is a challenge to the best that is in us. How worthy and wise objectives do challenge us! We have scarcely touched upon them here. An entire book might be well given to them alone. Surely, we want to find out more about them and how to achieve them. To this end may we not read and study some of the splendid books that will give us more assistance than this book can give because of its limitations of space?

V. We May Teach in Many Ways

It is, of course, not to be denied that the term "teaching" is often fairly employed in other senses than a technical one. Thus, we speak of teaching by our example, by the spirit which we manifest. Thus we lead others into the path we pursue, or impel them toward another path. Teaching of this kind, all of us engage in at all times; in this sense we are all teachers always. We are continually causing those about us to know and follow the better or the worse way, but it is not this kind of teaching that we have in mind when we say that we are teaching in Sunday school, or that we expect to teach next Sunday, or that we taught last Sunday. We have in mind active and purposeful teaching activities rather than what we may call our unconscious teaching (a teaching that is inevitable, whether we desire it or not), the inspiring and guiding of our pupils to learn what we know but what they do not know.

Teaching of this kind obviously involves the threefold idea of a teacher, objectives, and a learner. It involves desirable knowledge, attitudes, and skills which the teacher wants the learner to acquire along with a consciousness of his need of them. It also involves an actual leading of the learner to undergo the experiences that will result in his acquiring the necessary knowledge, attitudes, and skills before the teaching process is concluded. Hence, "teaching a lesson" includes the objectives proposed for that lesson, for unless there is learning by a learner there can be no teaching by a teacher, and until the teacher inspires and leads a learner to achieve these results, he has only tried to teach.

Classroom teaching is not all of a teacher's work. Teaching, in the sense that the term is usually employed, is by no means all of a teacher's work; nor is it always his most important work. His spirit, character, influence, and life may impress and influence his pupils as much or more than the instruction he gives. He should love his pupils and show it, sympathize with them and evidence it, gain their affections outside of the class as well as in it, and pray for them individually and in abiding faith. Thus will what he is and what he does during the week supplement and enrich his teaching efforts on Sunday. His knowledge of teaching principles, his ability to use good teaching methods, and his general knowledge and experience, will all be effective to the extent to which he has won the friendship and love of his pupils by having come to know them in their problems and needs. He will teach technically in the classroom through his good teaching methods; he will teach vitally in the classroom on Sunday and out of it during the week by his example. He will teach directly and indirectly, and in increasing effectiveness. He will give answer to the question, what is teaching, in the same way that an American poet has answered it in his tribute to Mark Hopkins:—

> Mark Hopkins sat on one end of a log,
>   And a farmer boy sat on the other
> Mark Hopkins came as a pedagogue
>   And taught as an elder brother.
> I care not what Mark Hopkins taught,
> If his Greek were small and his Latin naught,
>   For the farmer boy said, said he,
> All through lecture time and quiz,
>   'The kind of man I expect to be
> Is the kind of man Mark Hopkins is.'

VI. The Main Question at the End of the Lesson Period

The main question at the close of each Sunday school hour is not, were you with your class? not, did you prepare yourself on the facts of the lesson before coming to your class? not, did you state important truths which it was well for your class to know and then lead them to discuss these truths? not, were your hearers attentive, and seemingly impressed? but, did you lead the class through activities into experiences by which they came so to know and appropriate the truths of the lesson that they could and would go out and use them effectively in every-day living; did they come to know truth and make truth their own in a way to affect life and character? Until you can answer this question with positiveness, you cannot be sure that you have effectively taught the lesson or any part of it to all of your class or to any one pupil. Although teaching in the classroom is by no means the exclusive, nor yet always the foremost duty of a teacher, the test of teaching always rests with the learner, young or old, and not with the teacher. The teacher can prove that he tried to teach; the learner alone can show that the teacher really taught.

TEACHING SUGGESTIONS
Questions for Study and Review

1. What percentage of the teachers of your acquaintance do you think really teach? Do you teach?
2. Is telling teaching? Is telling a necessary part of the teaching process?
3. Is hearing a recitation teaching? What is the purpose of a recitation? What is its weakness as a means of teaching?
4. In what senses do teaching and learning have a common meaning?
5. Give three suggested phases of teaching and indicate the strength or weakness of each.
6. Indicate three kinds of teaching.
7. What four types of aims or objectives suggest the nature of our teaching?
8. Discuss the statement: "We may teach in many ways."
9. In what respect may teaching not be the teacher's most important task?
10. What is the main question at the end of the lesson?

Topical Outline

I. NEGATIVE APPROACH
   1. Telling is not teaching
   2. Hearing a recitation is not teaching

II. POSITIVE APPROACH
   1. "Learn" once used in twofold sense
   2. Teaching is one part of the twofold process

III. PHASES OF TEACHING
   1. Helping the pupil to learn
   2. Communication of truth
   3. Guiding growing life

IV. TEACHING IN THE LIGHT OF ITS AIMS
   1. Of three kinds
   2. Aims in teaching
      (1) Knowledge and Beliefs
      (2) Attitudes and Loyalties
      (3) Interests, Appreciations, and Ideals
      (4) Abilities and Skills

V. WE MAY TEACH IN MANY WAYS
   Classroom teaching not all of a teacher's work

VI. THE MAIN QUESTION AT END OF LESSON

III

TEACHERS SHOULD KNOW THEIR LEARNERS

Having considered the nature of the teaching process, let us look at some of its essential elements. We have seen that the teaching process is twofold, that it includes both teaching and learning, and that teaching requires, (1) a person to learn, (2) another person to aid him in his learning, and (3) what he is to learn. As for the teacher himself, he must know (1) whom he is to teach —the learner, (2) what he is to teach—the materials of instruction, such as lesson material, Bible, and so forth, and (3) how he is to teach—methods, procedures, techniques. To whatever extent he is deficient at any one of these three points, to that extent he will fail as a teacher.

In this chapter, let us consider the learner. In the next two chapters, we consider materials of instruction and teaching methods.

I. WHY TEACHERS SHOULD KNOW THEIR LEARNERS

Far too frequently, a teacher thinks that if he has mastered his subject matter (the lesson and related material) he is ready to teach. Not so; he needs to know his pupils or learners. The very nature of the teaching-learning process requires this, for teaching is the process by which the teacher helps his pupils to learn. But it is the pupils who must do the learning. How can the teacher help them to the best advantage if he does not really know them? If he wants to help them get rid of their ignorance, he must know the nature and extent of that ignorance. If he wants to help them acquire additional fruitful knowledge, he must know what knowledge they already have.

1. Words similar in meaning to teaching, if not its synonyms, are educate, edify, inform, instruct. Let us look at these four words.

(1) *Educate*. The deriviation of the word is significant: *e—duco*, to lead out. To educate is not primarily to pour in; rather, it is to draw out and develop, to cause that which is within to grow. But one must know what is within before he can cause to grow, or draw out and develop. In a word, the teacher must know the learner.

(2) *Edify*. The word suggests the building of an edifice within; but building edifices is a difficult and important business. How can one edify, build up, build edifices within, unless he knows what is within?

(3) *Inform*. The idea is to form within. It is not merely to pass on or pour in a mass of facts or ideas; rather, it is to form within. Again the necessity for the teacher to know the learner is implied.

(4) *Instruct*. Here the suggestion is to erect a structure within, to in-struct. If one would erect structures within people he must know them, what is in them, and what are their needs.

2. That the teacher must know the learner is evident from the product which both the teacher and the learner are to seek. In Chapter II it was made clear that teaching seeks as its objectives knowledge and beliefs, attitudes and loyalties, interests, appreciations and ideals, and abilities and skills.

(1) The teacher is to help his learners in acquiring knowledge and beliefs. To do this he must know as much as possible of both their ignorance and their knowledge. How else can he be a safe and inspiring guide?

(2) The teacher is to help his learners acquire and develop desirable attitudes and loyalties. He must, therefore, know his learners; know what are their attitudes and loyalties; know the source, the tenacity, the direction in which their attitudes and loyalties tend to develop.

(3) The teacher is to help his learners acquire and develop worthy interests, appreciations and ideals, but he can make no headway unless he knows what interests and appreciations and ideals his learners have already developed.

(4) The teacher is to help his learners acquire abilities and develop skills in Christian living. But to do this, he must know what abilities and skills his learners already have, and what abilities and skills they need to acquire.

A study of these elements of learning can only deepen the impression that the teacher must know his learners if he is to help them master knowledge, acquire beliefs, develop attitudes, grow loyalties, enrich interests, cherish appreciations, form ideals, achieve abilities, and develop skills.

The following story, told by Miss Margaret Slattery in her *Talks With the Training Class,* makes it clear that a teacher should know the pupils in his class.

Edith, who had been in her class for a few months was indifferent, and half-hearted in her attitude. As she neared her fourteenth birthday, Miss Slattery said to her, "Edith, your birthday comes next week, doesn't it?"

"Yes," she answered with a sigh; "I wish it didn't."

Miss Slattery was interested, and her questions elicited from the girl the statement: "You see I'm fourteen. I've got to leave school after this month. My brother got me a job in the factory and Father says I must go to work."

In the heart-to-heart talk which followed, Miss Slattery found out some interesting things. Her indifferent pupil was not indifferent after all. She really longed to go on to high school, and desired especially to study music. There was an organ in her home, but she had never taken a lesson. During these months, a really ambitious girl, she had dreaded the time when she would have to leave school. Commenting on this situation, Miss Slattery says significantly: "I had known Edith those months, of course; eyes, hair, voice, manner, general characteristics, and yet I had not known her at all. If I had, what might I not have made out of those few last months of school life! I suppose there have been many pupils whom I have not known. But my eyes have been opened since those first years."

II. What Teachers Should Know About Their Learners

If teaching is to be effective, the teacher must begin with the pupil or learner where he finds him. This means that the more he knows about the learner the more nearly he will be able to direct him in the learning process. It is not possible here to enumerate all that the teacher should know about the learner any more than it would be possible to state in advance all that the physician should know about his patient in order to minister properly to his physical well being. Here are some general suggestions that may help the teacher to know his learners.

1. *Know the Ignorance of Pupils*

Socrates said that a knowledge of our own ignorance is the first step toward true knowledge. Coleridge supplemented this truth with the suggestion that "we cannot make another comprehend our knowledge, until we first comprehend his ignorance." So long as a teacher supposes a learner to know what he does not know, the teacher is in no position to help him learn. Serious mistakes are constantly made in the Sunday school because of teachers' failure to know the ignorance of their learners.

An observant and faithful teacher was surprised by this question from a bright pupil about twenty-five years of age: "Who was the despised Galilean?" Another teacher taught lads of about fourteen, bright lads from cultured Christian homes. In one lesson, the difference between the teachings of Moses and Christ, the law and the gospel, was touched upon. The teacher questioned the lads as to their understanding of the terms "law" and "gospel." To his surprise, not one of them had any idea beyond a statutory civil law on the one hand, and the first four books of the New Testament on the other. Is it strange that there are absurd answers, or no answers at all, if learners do not better understand the words used in questioning them?

2. *Know the Vocabulary of Pupils*

All of us perhaps are using words continually in ordinary conversation which are not understood by those whom we address. A man once pointed out to his little daughter the beauty of the woods beyond the meadow which they were passing. The child looked puzzled but said nothing. When another reference was made to the woods, she ventured to ask: "Father, where are the woods? Are they back of those trees?" The meadow she knew, and the trees she knew, but where were the woods? She had never been told in so many words that a great number of trees together were called woods.

Children often lack a knowledge of things and an understanding of words with which they are supposed to be familiar. Professor G. Stanley Hall published the tabulated results of his careful examinations into the knowledge of common things possessed by some two hundred children who were just entering the Boston primary schools. Forty of them did not know their right hand, or their left; one out of three had never seen a chicken; two out of three had never seen an ant; one out of three had never consciously seen a cloud; two out of three had never seen a rainbow; more than half of them did not know that wooden things are made from trees; more than two-thirds of them could not tell what flour is made of; and so on through a long list of lesser and larger matters in the realm of common things. Professor Hall came to this conclusion: "There is next to nothing of pedagogic value, the knowledge of which it is safe to assume at the outset of school life."

Unless the Sunday school teacher tests the knowledge of his pupils at the point where he would begin his teaching, he is apt to underestimate their limitations, and thereby be unfitted to teach them wisely. All that has been said about the necessity of the teacher's knowing the limitations of the knowledge of his pupils applies to all pupils alike, children, youth, and adults.

3. *Know Each Pupil's Personality and Life*

The teacher should know his pupils, not only as to their knowledge and previous experiences, but also as to their tastes and peculiarities, their feelings and desires, their methods of thinking and modes of action, their characteristics and tendencies, their home life, and their week-day environment. It is related of Professor Orfila, the great French toxicologist, that when he was testifying in a court of justice of the relative power of minute doses of a particular poison, one of the lawyers in the case inquired of him derisively, "Could you tell us, Professor, the precise dose of this poison which a fly could take safely?" "I think I could," was the cautious answer; "but I should need to know something about the particular fly under treatment. I should want to know his size, his age, his state of health, his habits of life, whether he was married or single, and what had been his surroundings in life so far. All these things bear on the size of the dose to be administered in any case." Surely any one studying under our direction deserves as much study, and as wise and cautious treatment as a fly! But not every teacher is as wise or as cautious as was Professor Orfila.

Surely it is as important for a teacher to know his pupils as well as he knows the subject matter that he would use in teaching them. In fact, it is more important; and the mastery of knowledge about his pupils should precede or at least accompany his mastery of lesson material. Solomon's wisdom is evident at this point, for he said in substance that if each child is trained in the way that he should go—brought up with reference to his own particular needs, not those of children in general—he will not depart from that way in his adult life. This proverb's point is its emphasis upon giving a child individual training, not following general rules

which may not be adapted to him. "Instead of sanction-
ing a vigorous monotony of discipline under the notion
that it is 'the right way,' the proverb enjoins the closest
possible study of each child's temperament, and the adap-
tation of his way to that" (*The Speaker's Commentary*).
Training is a vital part of the larger teaching process,
and what is true of the part is true of the whole: teachers
must know their pupils individually to teach them effectively.

If a knowledge of the individual is so necessary for
effective teaching, why do teachers so often fail to study
their pupils and come really to know them for what they
actually are? Why do they not seek to know them one
by one with reference to their peculiarities, their prejudices, their understandings, their ways of thinking and
doing, their mental and spiritual habits? Is it because
it takes longer to learn people than it does to learn lesson material? because, being more difficult, it demands
more time, patience, and skill?

Many know how to master subject matter, but do not
know how to get a fair knowledge of those whom they
teach. One may have much learning, including a knowledge of principles and methods of teaching, and yet fail
largely as a teacher because he does not know his pupils
well enough to adapt his teaching to their individual
needs. Good intentions and piety and knowledge are
not enough; there must be the ability to see individual
differences and to adjust to them. Warm hearts and full
heads cannot atone for dull eyes which have a touch of
color-blindness, which see no real differences in the
shades which tinge the minds and dispositions of demure
and restless souls, of fun-loving youth and heavy-hearted
men and women, of those who have been home-taught
in Christian truth and those who were destitute of all
religious instruction before they entered the Sunday
school. To such a teacher, a class is a class, and a pupil
is a pupil; and every lesson is a series of facts to be taught
in one and the same way. And to every pupil and every
class, such a teacher is no teacher at all.

III. How Teachers May Know Their Learners

A study of the pupil in the abstract may have some value; a study of him in the concrete is better. A learned professor's specialty was child psychology. When he had some concrete paving laid, the neighbor children in a spirit of mischievous fun marred the smooth surface. The professor was much put out, and his wife chided him with, "I thought you liked children; you study and talk about them all of the time." He dryly replied, "I do like children; but I like them in the abstract, not in the concrete." But teachers must be interested in children and all people "in the concrete." They must take them and know them and love them as they are.

1. *Study Pupils Directly*

In all study of the class members individually, it is well to look for those characteristics and peculiarities which individualize them, which differentiate them from their immediate fellows. A teacher should consider the common characteristics of childhood, adolescence, and adulthood, and then the special characteristics of the age group that he teaches. In addition to this he should learn about the conditions that influence each learner in particular; for one cannot teach learners in general, but only one by one.

John Burroughs, in his essays on woodcraft, dwells on the necessity of having an eye to the "rare and characteristic things" in the trees and birds of the forest, if one would learn the truth about them separately. Then he tells of receiving letters, asking his aid in identifying the species of birds newly seen by his correspondents. In one case an extended description was given, without a single peculiar characteristic of the particular bird in question, for every feature named was common to a whole class of birds. In another case the few points noted, all peculiar and individual, enabled him to recognize the bird and name its species unhesitatingly.

Let a teacher select any one member of his class for consideration. Is he exceptionally bright, exceptionally dull, or of average intelligence? Is he familiar with the main points of the Bible story, through his home instruction or independent study, or is he ignorant of that record except as he has been taught it in the Sunday school? Is he forward of speech, ready to tell all that he knows, and readier to talk than to listen, or is he quiet and not inclined to speak out, even where he is well informed on a subject? Is he of a kindly or surly disposition, of a generous and manly nature, or of a selfish and unlovely spirit? Is he tender-hearted, quick to respond to any appeal to the feelings, or is he of a cold and sluggish temperament, not likely to be swayed by his emotions? Is he easily influenced by others, or has he marked independence of character? These and many similar questions may be answered by a teacher after a brief period of observation of the members of his class separately and in comparison with one another in the class; and answering them will go far toward giving him a knowledge of his learners individually.

But there are many things one needs to know which cannot be learned in the class or on Sundays; they must be ascertained during the week, and in or near the homes or places of employment, or, when the teacher and the pupil are by themselves in free social contact. Has the pupil a good home, or a wretched one? Is he the offspring of godly, high-minded parents, or parents whose influence is hurtful, or has he no parents living? Does he attend school? If so, what is his standing there? Has he some outside employment? If so, is he faithful or slack in its duties? Are his home and business and social surroundings such that they are in accord with the desired influence of the Sunday school, or against it? How does he spend his evenings and his other spare time? To what kind of reading does he incline? What temptations seem most to beset him? What seem to be the strongest inducements to his well-doing? What are his prevailing tastes and ambitions and weaknesses? If a teacher can get satisfactory answers to these questions, they will be invaluable to him.

2. *Study Pupils Indirectly*

Some things a teacher may find out about a pupil by his own observation; other things he may learn better through inquiry of, or contact with parents, or employers, or companions. The pupil is already known to some persons. Why should not the teacher profit by this knowledge that they have? Emerson says of the sure disclosure of one's character and characteristics under the observation of his sharp-eyed fellows: "The world is full of judgment days, and into every assembly that a man enters, and in every action that he attempts, he is gaged and stamped. In every troop of boys that whoop and run in each yard and square, a newcomer is well and accurately weighed in the course of a few days, and stamped with his right measure as if he had undergone a formal trial of his strength." Let the teacher profit from this common judgment which those who know his pupil best have passed upon him.

To pursue this study of his pupils in order to teach them intelligently makes a heavy demand on the teacher's time and ability; but he has no choice if he would teach them effectively. As to its importance and practicability a teacher says:

"With a class of twenty-five, and a busy daily life, I find time to know generally each one's daily work, and pretty largely his personal needs, so that Sunday finds me prepared for them separately, as well as for them as a class. The way I do it is twofold: first, by considering this duty quite as important and the work quite as necessary as my ordinary business; second, by encouraging my class to consult me about their daily troubles as well as about their spiritual needs."

3. *Study Pupils Through Experiences of People as Others Have Observed and Recorded Them*

Any teacher may learn much in general about those whom he teaches if he will take advantage of what others have put in writing about their experiences with and observations of people. Let him read books on psychology, some of which, by the way, are as interesting as good fiction. He may first read those written for Sunday school teachers because they are especially prepared for him; then he may read the more technical books which deal more thoroughly with mental and spiritual characteristics and processes and the way that personality grows or develops. Should he not try to read at least one good book on pupil life or psychology every year?

A teacher will find biographical books exceedingly helpful—biographies of biblical characters, missionaries, teachers, generals, statesmen, business men; biographies of Europeans, Americans, Negroes, Indians, and so forth; biographies in books and magazines; short and long biographies; new and old biographies. Many of them are more fascinating than fiction and also more valuable. Another good thing: they are cheap in price and available everywhere. How many of these ought a teacher to read every year—one, two, or more?

A teacher will take advantage of fiction, for some of the finest portrayals of character are to be found in novels and short stories. The novelist is free, not only to tell what his characters do, but also what they think and what their motives are. Fortunately, there are now available at popular prices books of choice fiction that deal with all types of persons, young and old, white and colored, rich and poor, learned and ignorant, wise and simple, good and bad, happy and sad. The teacher may well read at least two good books of fiction a year the better to learn human nature.

Finally, a teacher will read the daily and weekly papers and the monthly magazines, and religious papers and magazines for stories of human interest—news items, feature articles, editorials, and so forth. Thus, from systematic reading and study, any teacher can learn a great deal about people and use it in making a study of his own pupils.

4. *Recall Personal Experiences*

Recalling and analyzing one's own experiences is one of the best ways to understand human nature. Although introspection (looking within) has its limitations and dangers, one may best see others through his own experiences and understanding. If he has forgotten the incidents, experiences and motives of his own childhood, he ought not to teach children; and if he has forgotten those of his youth, he ought not to teach young people. An essential requirement of a good teacher is that he shall be able to enter into the experiences of his pupils with sympathy and understanding.

TEACHING SUGGESTIONS

Questions for Study and Review

1. What threefold knowledge is essential if the teacher is to teach?
2. What does the nature of the learning process suggest as to the necessity of knowing the learner?
3. Show how the words *educate, edify, inform* and *instruct* indicate the need of knowing the learner.
4. How do the aims sought in teaching show that the teacher must know the learner?
5. Is the story of Edith as related by Miss Slattery true to life? Show how Sunday school teachers may make similar mistakes.
6. Discuss some things which the teacher should know about his pupils.
7. Discuss briefly four methods of studying the pupils.

Topical Outline

I. WHY TEACHERS SHOULD KNOW THEIR LEARNERS

   1. Synonyms of teaching make it clear
   2. The aims sought emphasize it

II. WHAT TEACHERS SHOULD KNOW ABOUT THEIR LEARNERS
 1. Their ignorance
 2. Their vocabulary
 3. Their personality and life

III. HOW TEACHERS MAY KNOW THEIR LEARNERS
 1. Study them directly
 2. Study them indirectly
 3. Study them through experiences of other people
 4. Recall personal experiences

IV

TEACHERS SHOULD KNOW WHAT THEY WOULD TEACH

"I understand that you teach Latin," a man said to a college professor.

"No, that is a mistake," the professor replied, "I teach boys and girls."

In the same way it may be said that the Sunday school teacher does not teach the Bible, but children, or youths, or adults. But, as the word is generally used, the professor does teach Latin, and the Sunday school teacher does teach the Bible. These distinctions may be drawn, for truly, teachers teach persons instead of subject matter. Nevertheless, Sunday school teachers ought to know and teach the Bible.

I. Teachers Should Know the Bible

The Bible is the source book for Sunday school teaching. To it we must go, and from it we must draw, as we face the members of our class week by week. Better still, we are to inspire and guide our learners in their own efforts to explore and understand the way of life as they find it set forth in the Bible. We are to study our learners to find what they need, and then go to the Bible to get it. The Bible is a tool for use in building Christian character.

This is all true; but it is not the full truth. The Bible is more than a source book from which we are to draw. It is more than a wonderfully helpful book in whose exploration we are to lead our learners. It is more than a tool for use in teaching. It is itself a divine book, a dynamic book. It sets forth and supplies what both we and our learners need. "The word of God is living and active, and sharper than any two-edged sword, and piercing even to the dividing of soul and spirit, of both joints and marrow, and quick to discern the thoughts and intents of the heart" (Heb. 4:12 ASV). Therefore we are to teach, and our pupils are to learn, the Bible. It offers a revelation of God; it brings a message of salvation from sin and death; it is a guide to holy living. If we fail to teach it, if our pupils fail to learn it, we fail utterly.

However much or little of the Bible a teacher may be asked to teach to his class, it is necessary that he should know his Bible. The more fully and deeply he knows it, the more fully and deeply can he teach the particular portions that may be given him to teach.

1. *Know the Words and Facts of the Bible.* There are certain parts of the Bible whose words every teacher should know so that he can repeat them readily and accurately. We hear much of the importance of memorizing passages of scripture. Sometimes it seems to be assumed that the mere fact that one can repeat much of the Bible will necessarily result in spiritual growth. This assumption does not rest upon a sound basis. In fact, there is convincing proof that mere verbal memory is no indication of real learning. However, to know the words of the Bible, words that have been made a part of experience, is quite another thing. Such knowledge makes it possible for the teacher to use the Bible with ease. There are many Bible facts which he should know, such as the names and order of the books, the general content of the books, the authors, the sweep of the unfolding history, the characters, and other similar information.

2. *Know the Teachings of the Bible.* Down beneath the words and the facts lies the real Bible. Here is its message of revelation. The words and facts constitute the medium through which God speaks to man concerning truth and life and redemption. And, while they are remarkably plain and simple, they become clear only through study and meditation.

3. *Have an Experimental Knowledge of the Bible.*
The message and revelation of the Bible should be so
accepted, believed, and lived that they become one's own
possession, a part of one's inner self. We may know
the words and facts of the Bible without knowing their
meaning and teaching. We may also know much of the
meaning and teaching without accepting their challenge
or vitally receiving their deeper message. In fact, we
do not really know the Bible unless and until we know
it experimentally. It must be ours in the changes it
works, in the experiences it produces, ours in that having
been wrought into our life it bears fruit in our character
and daily conduct.

II. How Teachers May Know the Bible

It is more important that a teacher be a growing Bible
student than that he shall be a finished Bible scholar.
When he ceases to acquire and enrich his biblical knowledge, he ceases to do real, creative Bible teaching. He
should, therefore, be a constant, faithful, intelligent student of the Bible. Not many teachers can pursue Bible
courses in Christian colleges and seminaries, but all can
individually and collectively engage in practical and
helpful study of it.

1. *Read the Bible Devotionally.* Every teacher needs
food for his own spiritual life. He needs direct contact with God, and a daily, prayerful, meditative reading will give him this contact. He will usually want
to use his favorite version, but he may get much help
from reading also in some of the modern translations,
especially some of the translations of the New Testament.

2. *Study the Bible by Books.* One of the most helpful
ways to study the Bible, especially the New Testament,
is by books. Each letter or epistle, for example, was
a separate document, and most epistles were written to
a group of Christians at some particular place to help
them personally. Most books of the Bible are brief

and can be covered profitably in a relatively short time. Many excellent helps are available for this type of study.

3. *Study Books on the Bible.* There are a number of helpful books of this type in the Sunday School Training Course—introductory, historical, biographical, expository. These may be studied at home or in a class. Directions for study are given in each book.

Besides these, teachers should study books on the life of Christ, the life of Paul, the lives of other Old and New Testament characters. There are many volumes that will help in this field.

Besides books on the Bible, there are books on portions of the Bible—the Ten Commandments, the Sermon on the Mount, the Beatitudes, the Lord's Prayer, the parables, the miracles, and so forth.

4. *Study Books About the Bible.* For one to really know his Bible he must learn much *about* the Bible. It was written in languages now extinct, and to people who lived from two to four thousand years ago. It abounds in allusions and references that are strange to us. The customs and ways of thinking of its people were vastly different from our customs and ways of thinking. The writers did not need to make explanations and give information that we must have if we are to understand what they wrote. Those to whom they wrote did not need the explanations and information. We can get the needed information only by consulting scholars who have studied long and faithfully. The undying truths and eternal principles of the Bible were given to the people of long ago to help them with their moral and spiritual problems. Teachers need to know how to work through the habits and customs, the ways of thinking and doing, and the problems of those far-off people to get hold of those undying truths and eternal principles, so that they may make them available for their pupils in solving their own moral and spiritual problems.

There are many interesting and helpful medium-priced books about the Bible—commentaries, concordances, harmonies of the Gospels, Bible dictionaries, Bible atlases and geographies, books on Bible manners and customs, how we got our Bible, history of the English Bible, individual translations of the Bible, history of Jewish people in New Testament times, and so forth.

5. *Study the Sunday School Lessons.* Regardless of whether a teacher uses the Uniform or the Graded Lessons, he should study thoroughly the biblical passages selected for the weekly lesson, not only that he may teach effectively, but also that he may better know his Bible. The use of either of these series through a year or period of years, constitutes an excellent means of systematic Bible study.

If a teacher uses the Uniform Lessons for teaching Juniors, Intermediates, Young People or Adults, he should study, not only his teacher book, but also the quarterly furnished his pupils. For further enrichment he may use helps such as the *Broadman Comments and others,* read the lesson treatments in daily and weekly papers, and listen to their discussion over the radio.

If he uses the Graded Lessons, he usually teaches the same series of lessons year after year. Besides mastering the biblical material in these lessons, which may be limited to definite selections, he may study additionally the Uniform Lessons. Each five-year cycle of Uniform Lessons carries one through the historical portions of the Old Testament, at least partially through the writing prophets and through each of the Four Gospels, Acts, the life of Paul, of Peter, and of John, and also several series of topical studies.

(1) *The Advantages of Lesson Helps.* Lesson helps are useful because they provide a systematic series of lessons for the pupils to study. They are also of great value to the teacher in mastering the Bible, for they bring him at a very reasonable price and in useful form the reverent scholarship of the world and make it available just where and when he most needs it. Most teachers are busy people, and many of the books they need for

studying the Bible they do not have. What a blessing to them are these helps which are themselves prepared by thoughtful professors, scholary pastors, successful Sunday school teachers, and trained editorial writers. Practically all of those who prepare these helps are themselves Sunday school teachers.

(2) *Possible Disadvantages of Lesson Helps.* Lesson helps are positively harmful when a teacher comes to depend on them too much and does not study his Bible and utilize other sources of knowledge. They are prepared to guide the teacher in studying the Bible; they ought not to supplant his study of it.

Those who prepare lesson helps are themselves but students of the Bible. They are not infallible interpreters. Teachers must therefore guard against too readily accepting what the lesson writers and editors say. They must increasingly learn how to do their own thinking and reach their own conclusions.

III. Teachers Should Know Each Lesson

It takes a lifetime to learn the Bible in a really adequate manner, for its riches are inexhaustible. A teacher cannot wait until he masters Bible knowledge, for he must teach next Sunday, and the week after that, and so on week after week. And there is a definite, particular lesson for each week, with its title, its biblical material, its lesson aim, and so forth. Surely, then, he must know each week the particular lesson that he is to teach. To know it, he must not only master the lesson material in the Bible; he must also know what there is in that lesson that his pupils in particular need to know.

One may ask him, "What are you going to teach?" He may reply, "I am going to teach Bible truth." The answer is indefinite, for there is so much truth involved that he cannot teach it all at one lesson period.

He may therefore repeat his question, "What are you going to teach," to which the reply may be, "I am going to teach next Sunday's lesson."

"Even so, but what is next Sunday's lesson?" If he answers, "Mark 5:21-42," the questioner is still in doubt, for the teacher has only given the location of the passage that is to be taught. If he replies, "The subject of the lesson is 'Power over Disease and Death,'" he has merely given the subject of the lesson in the lesson helps. If he says, "I am going to get my pupils to understand and appreciate the power of Jesus to heal the sick and raise the dead as it is revealed in Mark 5:21-42," and if he then goes on to mention several facts in Jesus' life which reveal his knowledge as well as his power, and comments on the spirit of faith which Jesus approved—if he says all this, the questioner will have assurance that the teacher knows what he is going to teach.

To know a lesson, the teacher must master the facts of the lesson, including places, dates, times, manners, customs, conversation, discussion, events. He may say, "I look upon some of these as of minor importance." If so, what does he consider important? Will he teach the mere words and ask the pupils only to recite them?

He must master the meaning of the facts, understand the teachings or doctrines involved, and know the value of a practical application of both facts and teachings to the problems of life. He must also know the facts and teachings with reference to the needs of his pupils, and how to get the pupils to lay hold of and use them.

Unless and until the teacher so learns the lesson that he is to teach on a given Sunday, he does not really know, he has not actually mastered, the lesson.

IV. TEACHERS SHOULD KNOW ADDITIONAL SUBJECT MATTER

"Out of the abundance of the heart the mouth speaketh" (Matthew 12:34). So spake the Lord Jesus. Out of the abundance of knowledge the teacher teacheth; he must know more than he needs to use at one lesson period, else he could not select. He may know his biblical material, and the material in the lesson helps. The lesson helps are necessarily limited, and they may not contain some things which are very necessary if he is to teach his pupils effectively.

God is still in his world. The Holy Spirit still guides and empowers men. It will soon be nineteen hundred years since the last book of the New Testament was written. What has happened to the succeeding generations of Christians?

It will be exceedingly helpful to a teacher if he can have a fair knowledge of church history, and the history of his denomination. Surely he should know as much as possible about the history of missions and be familar with the lives of outstanding Christian thinkers and scholars and preachers and missionaries and teachers and statesmen and other men and women of note. And should he not want to learn as much as possible of the influence of the Bible on civil and criminal law, codes of ethics, architecture, music, painting, literature? All of this knowledge will enrich him personally and increase his effectiveness in teaching every lesson. Knowledge of the Bible, knowledge about the Bible, knowledge of each lesson, and all other enriching knowledge will the teacher need for his teaching. Truly, there is no limit to what a person may learn; and he can and must always begin right where he is, here a little, there a little, line upon line.

TEACHING SUGGESTIONS

Questions for Study and Review

1. In what sense do we teach the Bible?
2. Indicate some ways in which the teacher must know the Bible.
3. How may teachers come to know the Bible?
4. What are the advantages of lesson helps? What are possible disadvantages?
5. What is it for a teacher to know a given lesson?
6. Discuss some "additional subject matter" with which the teacher should be acquainted.

Topical Outline

I. TEACHERS SHOULD KNOW THE BIBLE
1. The words and facts
2. The teachings
3. Have an experimental knowledge of it

II. HOW TEACHERS MAY KNOW THE BIBLE
1. Read it devotionally
2. Study it by books
3. Study books on the Bible
4. Study books about the Bible
5. Study the Sunday school lessons

III. TEACHERS SHOULD KNOW EACH LESSON

IV. TEACHERS SHOULD KNOW ADDITIONAL SUBJECT MATTER

V

TEACHERS SHOULD KNOW HOW TO TEACH

Even when one possesses the essential knowledge about his pupils, and has full knowledge of the desired objectives and the material to be used in the teaching, he is still unprepared to bear his part in the twofold teaching-learning process unless he knows how to teach. With his class before him and well understood by him, and with the truth which he purposes to teach in his mind, the question remains, How will he proceed to direct the work of the class period in order to develop the desired understandings on the part of his learners?

In everything that needs doing, a knowledge of the method of doing it is of prime importance. A man cannot milk a cow, or whitewash a fence, or mend a shoe, or write a book, or do anything effectively without knowing how. The fact that the work is religious does not make it any less important that the one responsible for it should know how to do it. He who would preach must know how to preach, and he who would teach in the Sunday school must know how to teach. He must not only be acquainted with wise methods of teaching that have been developed through successful experience; he must also develop plans in accordance with those methods for the work immediately before him.

Various methods of procedure are used in teaching. Not all teachers can use the same method, nor are all methods alike suited to every class. Each teacher must use the methods which, all things considered, enable him best to teach his own pupils. For him it is not so much, what are the different approved methods? not, what method is most commonly successful? but, what method shall I use in teaching this lesson to my class? How may I best help my pupils to understand and use the lesson truths which have meaning to me and which I want them to get hold of in a vital way? What activities must I engage in as a teacher in order that my pupils may learn most effectively?

Teacher activities in directing learning may be of various kinds. When we refer to activity we do not limit our meaning to overt physical action. In fact, under certain conditions an appropriate activity for the teacher may be simply to "do nothing." Once a wise teacher kept perfectly quiet under conditions which would have caused most teachers to react vigorously. He was trying to develop a spirit of reverence. Most of the pupils were responsive, but one pupil showed his contempt for what the teacher and the class were trying to do. Instead of reproving the offender the teacher "did nothing." The other pupils showed their disapproval so distinctly that their fellow pupil was chagrined and humiliated. A wise teacher knows when "doing nothing" is an appropriate activity. Specific rules or directions cannot be given him in advance without limiting his work, but various procedures for selecting and organizing class activities may be suggested.

The question therefore, becomes, What may a teacher do to help his pupils learn most effectively? Certainly, no one type of procedure can be followed, for conditions and situations differ. However, some general types of procedure have been developed from the experiences of successful teachers. They fall into three groups: (1) initiating the lesson, (2) developing the lesson, and (3) concluding the lesson. It should be recognized, however, that conditions under which Sunday school teaching usually takes place tend to restrict a teacher to a much more formal and direct process than he would follow if he had more time and freedom. The suggestions that follow are made with these restrictions in mind.

I. INITIATING (BEGINNING) THE LESSON

Much depends upon the beginning of a lesson period. Assuming that the teacher has the facts and other materials well in hand, how shall he begin? The details will vary, of course, with the age and the social, mental, and spiritual maturity of the learners. However, regardless of the nature of the group to be taught, a point of common group interest must be found and utilized as an immediate stimulus to action. This may be done in a number of ways, but the teacher should be careful to avoid a stereotyped plan to be used Sunday after Sunday.

1. *By Question.* One of the most familiar ways to begin is to ask a question. Some teachers invariably begin in this manner. If a question is asked, it should be carefully related to the interests and needs of the group and should be used to stimulate further interest. Such questions as, what is the subject of today's lesson, and, where is our lesson passage for today found, rarely make a strong beginning. Occasionally, particularly with adults, such a question may be asked, provided the lesson title or subject has a special significance.

Questions for initiating a lesson period should be so phrased and asked that they will stimulate immediate interest and secure a response to other questions and answers, or discussions by the class. They should tend to direct the thought and activity of the class in the direction indicated by the objectives the teacher has in mind.

2. *By Suggestion.* One of the most effective ways for beginning a class period is for the teacher to make a statement or suggestion that is calculated to stimulate discussion by the members of the class. There is often a strong temptation for the teacher to make a radical or extreme statement in order to secure attention. This is a sort of trick or device that may seem to be effective because, for the moment, it appears to command the undivided attention of the group. However, as a rule, such catch statements are so far removed from the real

work of the class hour that the shift to the main consideration is too abrupt. Consequently the effort is often
lost so far as the main purpose is concerned.

3. *By Question or Suggestion from a Pupil.* Another
effective way to initiate a good learning situation is for
a pupil to ask a question or make a suggestion. The pupil
should know beforehand what he is to ask or suggest and
the reason for it. Otherwise a rambling and irrelevant
discussion may result. If an irrelevant or undesirable
discussion does develop, the teacher must as tactfully
as possible bring it to an end and return to more vital
matters.

4. *By Presenting a Person or Some Object of Interest.*
There is a large range of possibilities at this point. The
presentation of persons who for some reason may arouse
the interest of the class provides a very effective open-
ing. A local hero, a person who has had an unusual
experience, some one who has recently come into promi-
nence—these are always possibilities. It is not often wise
to turn the whole class period over to such a person.
Sometimes the visitor lacks the ability to carry on the
work of the class period successfully—talks too much,
or does not speak interestingly, or runs along aimlessly
without regard to time and thus loses the benefit of the
climax at the close of the class period. The teacher
should never turn the class period over to some one else
unless he is certain that the time will be used effectively.

Sometimes, when an interesting visitor is invited to
attend the class meeting, it is desirable to turn the first
part of the hour into a very informal meeting wherein
the visitor and the members of the class ask and answer
questions of common interest. The teacher should see to
it that, as far as possible, the discussion gives opportunity for developing the central thought or main objective planned for the lesson period.

There is almost an endless variety of objects that may
be used to stimulate interest and provide the initiation of
a good learning situation. Books, pictures, and objects

of peculiar construction or of special historic interest present abundant possibilities for bringing the members of a class together around a common center of interest. We repeat here, the interest must be such that it can easily lead to the development of the activities of the class in the direction of the desired objectives which the teacher has in mind.

A good way to judge an initial class activity is its effectiveness in leading the pupils to follow through to a satisfactory conclusion. Any beginning, however modest, that does this is a successful beginning; any beginning, however attractive in itself, that does not do this is an unsuccessful beginning.

II. Developing the Lesson

The teacher makes a beginning in which the members of the class develop a purpose to carry through the class activities in the direction indicated by his aims. There remains the task of developing such activities as will bring out the meaning of the discussed truths and make them real and personal to the learners. This, if done successfully, requires activity on the part of both teacher and learners. Here again, it is not possible to indicate any single method for all or even most occasions. No set formula should be followed, for the maturity of the learners and many other conditioning factors must be taken into account.

Various effective methods of developing a lesson have been used by successful teachers and are here presented briefly. To consider them at all we have to take them up in succession, but we need to guard ourselves against thinking that they mutually exclude one another. Frequently, the best results may be secured by using several of them during one lesson period. For example, a teacher may give the lecture method pre-eminence, but he will almost certainly use the method more effectively by weaving in questions and answers, periods of discussion, and effective story-telling. His skill consists in part in knowing how to use the several methods to achieve a consistent and unified teaching process. We need to learn how to use methods effectively. There are many good books on teaching, both for the public school and the Sunday school that will help us to do this.

1. *By Questions and Answers.* Questions are not only useful in initiating a lesson; they may help much in developing it. They should be used, not only to find out whether the pupils have mastered the lesson material, but also to provoke thought and guide discussion. There is an art in asking questions. Skill is necessary to use them successfully. It is not easy to ask direct, pointed, clear questions which the pupils will understand.

Questions may be used effectively in connection with the solution of a problem. A problem may be stated, and then some one may be asked what he thinks about it. When he answers, another may be asked what he thinks of the answer. If the class members are willing to accept an answer as satisfactory when it is not, the teacher may ask such questions as these, Have you taken this into consideration? or, What will you do with this? or, How, then, do you explain this?

Often the answer to a question leads logically to another question or a series of questions. An answer should usually involve more than a simple yes or no. If it is incorrect, questions will show whether the other members of the class accept the answer as correct. If partially correct, other questions may be asked to help the pupil answer more fully, or to guide other pupils in giving a more complete answer. The teacher should not often tell a pupil that he has answered incorrectly. Instead, he should ask other questions to help him see wherein he has failed, or get other pupils to complete the answer.

2. *By Conversation.* If the class is small (not more than eight or ten) the teacher may effectively use informal conversation for developing the lesson. He should lead it, keep it related to whatever problems he wishes

to consider, and encourage his pupils to talk frankly and
without any feeling of embarrassment. A conversation
does not require as much study to be successful as a discussion, but it may help to train the class for discussion.

3. *By Discussion.* One of the most effective methods
for developing a lesson is through discussion. The teacher
should plan for it, initiate it and keep it going by tactful
questions and helpful comments. He should be careful
not to talk too much himself, and he must guide and
control or the class will get away from the lesson and the
problem. If when planning the lesson, he thinks that a
discussion will be helpful, he may designate one or more
to lead it, acquaint them with what he wants discussed,
and if possible put them in touch with other material
than that which they themselves possess. A discussion
may be directed towards acquiring facts and information,
coming to a clearer understanding of a subject, inter-
preting the lesson material, developing a doctrine or
teaching, or determining how principles involved may be
made effective in some area of conduct or in solving some
problem of daily living.

The teacher must not let a few monopolize the discussion. He should recognize one who has not entered into
the discussion in preference to one who has already taken
an active part. He should reserve enough time to sum
up the discussion, help the class to see what they have
achieved and realize that the discussion has been really
profitable. If it is of a creative nature, it will probably
suggest further problems that need discussing. If so,
the teacher may at once make suggestions for an
adjourned class session so that the members may prepare
to carry the discussion further.

Sometimes, when a discussion on a vital topic waxes
warm and there is a clearly defined difference of opinion,
with good leaders on both sides, a continuance of the discussion may more nearly approximate a debate. The
teacher may designate a leader for each side and suggest
that the two select one or two to aid them. The teams
may then engage in further study and work together for

the presentation of their side of the subject. In this event, the teacher may serve as coach to both sides, and then preside at some special meeting of the class, being careful to see that the debate is conducted in the right spirit and with proper feeling and with an honest desire to reach conclusions that will be spiritually helpful to all. Under these conditions, desirable outcomes may be expected.

4. *By Lecture.* Teachers often develop the lesson by lecturing. Because it may call for less work by the teacher in getting ready for the class session, and makes less demands on the pupils, the lecture is more widely and frequently used than is desirable. Teachers may mistakenly assume that their lectures are effective because of the quietness of the class and their seeming attention and interest. They need to make sure, too, that they are really teaching through the lecture, not merely telling, or giving information, or doing special pleading. At times, particularly with an adult class, the teacher may make thorough preparation and present in an orderly manner a body of carefully selected material and interpret it with good results. If a teacher lectures, he should prepare carefully what he wants to say to his class, and then present it so that it will be effective teaching, teaching that will result in the desired learning by the members of his class. At all events, he should give time for the class to ask questions and to discuss whatever may call forth more or less dissent. Thus the so-called lecture will in reality become a co-operative discussion.

5. *By Using the Story.* Fortunate indeed is the teacher who can tell a story well in developing the lesson. He must know how to adapt the story to his teaching and get the class to see its appropriateness. It may be very brief or it may take a good portion of the period. Whatever its length, the teacher should make sure that he knows how to tell it effectively. Having told it, he should know how to use it for developing a conversation

or discussion that will help him to achieve his aim or purpose.

The use of the story links up closely with the use of illustrations of an anecdotal nature. Good anecdotes, well told and aptly used, often help in making a point, clearing up a misunderstanding, or driving home a truth. One who is skilled in telling them may be tempted to use them too often and when they have no real relation to the topic under discussion.

6. *By Dramatization.* Although people of all ages like to take part in a play, dramatization is an especially effective means of developing a lesson with younger pupils. It is essential that the class have a genuine interest in the material to be presented, and that as many members as possible participate in some phase of it. Selecting and planning what is to be presented, arranging it in dramatic form, selecting the characters, providing scenery and costumes,—all of these offer possible activities that will engage the interest of various members of the class. Tact must be used to see that no one feels that he has been "left out." All activities should be so directed that they will help in the attainment of desirable objectives. It is a mistake to have a dramatization unless it is definitely a teaching activity. Except in abbreviated form, dramatizations are not suitable for brief class sessions. They may be used effectively in special meetings of the class.

7. *By Experience Units.* Various names have been used to indicate a type of learning situation in which the members of the class engage in some worthwhile activity that extends beyond the limits of a single class period. Such terms as "project," "contract," or "activity unit" are frequently used in educational literature to designate it. In Sunday school a "community project" is often an effective means of developing a lesson of the experience unit type. A variety of activities may be engaged in by both teacher and pupils. The objectives should be made clear to all who participate, plans made for carrying the

enterprise through, and responsibility assigned for its various phases.

A group of boys, participating in a boys' hobby fair, were attracted by the wide variety of interesting models displayed. The teacher took advantage of this interest and directed the attention of one boy to the specifications for Solomon's temple as detailed in Second Kings. Other members of the class became interested. Soon, plans were under way for building a model. This required careful reading of relevant Scripture passages and other source material. Plans were drawn to scale, and portions of the work were assigned to different boys. Interest became intense. One member of the class was relied upon to become an authority on the construction, another on the use and the significance of the Temple, and another on the historical events that occurred in connection with its building and destruction. After several weeks the model was completed and placed on exhibition. A dedication service was then held. As the visitors examined the model, the boys explained its significance. Needless to say, the boys had read the Scripture passages not as mere assignments, but purposefully because of their interest. Certainly they learned more of the Bible during this project than they would have learned otherwise. Such teaching of course takes for granted special outside sessions of a Sunday school class.

Care must be exercised in directing such an activity to see that the mere construction phase does not become an end in itself. The whole enterprise should be used to achieve definite spiritual objectives.

Seven possible steps or phases in developing a lesson have been offered and discussed. As has already been said, they are not to be considered methods of teaching. No one of them alone can be thought of as a method of presenting a lesson. Rather the teacher will use several of them, possibly all of them, and possibly other steps as well, as he makes up his complete plan for developing the lesson.

III. Concluding the Lesson

It is not enough to initiate and develop a lesson properly; it must also be carried through to a successful conclusion. A good teacher will reserve some time to sum up what has occurred. Teacher and pupils together will evaluate or judge the results of the activities engaged in during the lesson period. If questions remain unanswered, provision will be made for further consideration at a later class period. If there are apparent problems with individual members of the class, the teacher should tactfully arrange to continue the discussion immediately if possible so as to resolve the difficulty. If this cannot be done, then the next problem should be given further consideration at the next class meeting. In concluding a class period it is desirable to secure from members of the class some expression as to their application of the truths that have been considered. Often a brief silent prayer gives opportunity for the significance of a lesson to become effective. Care should be exercised to see that no extraneous matter is introduced during the closing moments of a class period. To do so often serves to disrupt a train of thought and to dissipate largely the results that have been developed during the lesson period.

If he has not done so before, the teacher should direct attention to the subject for the next lesson, make suggestions that will help the class to master the lesson material, make assignments to at least some of the pupils for definite work that he wishes them to do, and show the relation of the next subject to the one that has just been considered.

Much of this discussion of methods has necessarily assumed that classes will hold adjourned sessions Sunday afternoons or during week days. All lesson courses provided for the Sunday school comprise continuous and progressive studies which make it desirable that each lesson shall be studied in its proper place unless some special condition makes it necessary to introduce some other lesson.

TEACHING SUGGESTIONS

Questions for Study and Review

1. Why is a study of method in teaching necessary?
2. Can all teachers use the same methods? Why?
3. Into what groups do the procedures of lesson preparation fall?
4. Indicate with brief discussion some methods of beginning a lesson. Which of these do you most frequently use?
5. List with brief discussion the seven suggested phases of developing a lesson. Which of these phases do you most often use?
6. Indicate some ways in which the lesson may be closed.

Topical Outline

I. INITIATING THE LESSON

    1. By question
    2. By suggestion
    3. By question or suggestion from a pupil
    4. By presenting a person or object of interest

II. DEVELOPING THE LESSON

    1. By questions and answers
    2. By conversation
    3. By discussion
    4. By lecture
    5. By using the story
    6. By dramatization
    7. By experience units

III. CLOSING THE LESSON

VI

TEACHERS SHOULD SECURE AND USE THE INTEREST OF THEIR LEARNERS

The teacher is in the presence of his pupils with the objectives he desires to achieve in mind; he has a clear and well-defined understanding of the meaning of the facts or materials through which he wishes his pupils to achieve the desired objectives; and he has a well-defined plan of teaching. All this preparedness, however, will amount to but little unless he can enlist the interest and secure the active attention of his pupils.

A great deal has been said and written about the importance of securing and holding the attention of the learner. It is true that there is and can be no learning, and therefore no teaching, without attention. Various means have been suggested for securing and holding attention. However, attention is too often taken to be something that can be induced from without and can be sustained by artificial means. As a rule, the means suggested for securing and holding attention consist of some startling statement, some unusual question, some curious object, or, weakest of all, a direct request for attention. When it is secured by such external means, attention is usually of short duration and is not conducive to learning, however quiet and apparently interested the members of the class may be.

Teaching is not so simple a process as may be implied in the admonitions to secure and hold attention of the learner. To assume that attention can be induced by artificial means and can be sustained by forces outside the individual learner is not in accord with the best thought and experience regarding the nature of learning. Attention is but an indication of something deeper. It is the immediate result of interest, an interest that is vital and active. We tend to overlook the very basis of teaching when we treat attention as merely one of several more or less mechanical steps in the teaching-learning process.

I. Learning an Active Process

As has been stated previously, learning is an active process. This does not mean that the learner must engage in overt physical activity, for reading, observing, listening, meditating, discussing, and constructing are activities in the sense in which the term is used in teaching. Monroe says: "It is only through engaging in activities that the child learns. The teacher cannot communicate skills, ideas, facts, principles, and ideals directly to the student; knowledge is not transferred from a textbook to the learner's mind." Considered from this point of view, then, there is no such thing as passive learning. This holds true not only for the child but for the adult as well, although physical activity is of much greater significance in the learning of children than of adults.

Since learning is an active process, the task of the teacher becomes that of directing the activities of his learners so that the desired objectives will be achieved. We must not conclude, however, that just any activity in which the pupil may engage will result in the desired learning. Some schools of thought imply that it makes but little difference what activities the learner engages in so long as he is busy. Any passing fancy, mistaken for genuine interest, may result in more or less meaningless activity. The activities in which the learner engages must be purposeful. They must be engaged in to the end that the learner may achieve his own purpose. The work of the teacher is to bring the learner's purpose to coincide as nearly as possible with his own aims or objectives. Once a learner develops a worthy purpose, attention will largely take care of itself. To achieve his purpose the learner may feel the need of the facts contained in a certain Bible narrative, a knowledge of the experience of some character, the words of a text of Scripture, or an interpretation of some passage or event by the teacher. Whatever purpose a pupil may develop, attention to learning activities will normally follow until he achieves his purpose or develops another.

II. Developing Worthy Purposes

We are all constantly engaged in some sort of activity actuated by some purpose. The purposes of the members of a Sunday school class may be, and probably are, quite varied. Some members attend to meet and visit with their friends; some, to receive the approval of the teacher, of the pastor, or of friends; others, to avoid the criticism or censure of parents or of neighbors. Some purpose to learn more of the truth of the Bible, and so on. Out of this medley of purposes the teacher must find some common center of interest around which he may develop a common purpose, and then stimulate and direct those activities that help the members to realize their purpose. There may be good teaching when all members of the group do not have the same interest and are not moved by the same purpose. In fact, it might be possible to teach if every member of the class had a different purpose, but this would call for a variety of activities difficult to provide within the limits in which Sunday school teaching usually takes place. Moreover, co-operative activities of the several pupils around a common purpose provide opportunities for many desirable learning situations. Many an attempt to teach has failed because the teacher felt that he could not proceed unless every member of the class was "paying attention" in exactly the same way.

Purpose has its basis in the interest of the learner. It naturally follows that the purposes of the learners vary with their interests. With a younger group their purposes reflect interests that are stimulated by their immediate environment. They may purpose to dramatize some entracing Bible story, or construct some object in which their interest has been stimulated. The interests of more mature learners, who have a broader view of the meaning and purpose of the Sunday school, may develop in them the purpose to analyze a selected text of Scripture, or examine some fundamental doctrine, or apply some Bible teaching to a problem of current social interest. Such a variety of purposes growing out of a variety of interests calls for varying degrees of application on the part of the learners and, hence for many types of activities extending over varying periods of time.

III. UTILIZING INTERESTS

The point of beginning for the teacher is found in the interests of the members of his class. Jesus, the master Teacher, gives us numerous examples of good teaching when he seizes upon some item of intense personal interest in his learner and presses home some vital truth. One day some men asked him, "Rabbi, where dwellest thou?" He replied, "Come and see." They followed him and learned many precious truths concerning his character and the nature of his kingdom. Once he asked for a drink of water of a Samaritan woman who had come to the well with her pitcher and was therefore interested in water. Soon she was seeking eagerly to learn about "the living water." Jesus took people as he found them. He recognized their interests, and from these he led them to seek to know more of him and his everlasting truth.

IV. AROUSING MENTAL ATTITUDES

Much of the teaching in the Sunday school does not involve problem solving, because of the difficulty of maintaining continuity of interest and action when only a thirty or forty minute class period is available for the teacher and class to solve their problems. Because of this limitation of time a teacher must adopt other means to develop interest in the Bible truth which he would teach, such as the use of stories and pictures and songs and so forth. Preparatory to such teaching he endeavors to arouse a general mental attitude—expectancy, curiosity, playfulness, for example—by recalling certain trains of thought which contain good suggestions for introducing the material to be studied. These attitudes have their basis in the interest of the learner.

It has been said that the teacher must know his learner. He must, therefore, keep informed about what engages his learner's interest. The wise teacher studies the common interests of his pupils. He also tries to find what is of immediate interest to each pupil.

One may learn much about the common interests of pupils of a given age group by studying books that have been written about them. The authors of such books have gone to great pains to observe and record the predominating interests of learners of various ages. Such lists of interests should be studied and supplemented by careful observation. Thus one may see that boys of a certain age are usually interested in "making things," and that another group are interested in athletics and physical prowess. All these interests, having been carefully noted, should be used by the teacher as a guide in planning for the activities of his pupils.

V. CATALOGING INTERESTS

Numerous classifications of types of interest have been made. One list, based upon the so-called instinctive interests, illustrates how a check list may be made, and suggests its possible use:—

Interest in adventure and romance.
Interest in actions of people and animals.
Desire for social approval.
Interest in rhythm, rime, jingle, and song.
Curiosity, wonder, puzzle interest, problem interest.
Interest in expression and communication.
Manipulation and general physical activity.
Collecting.
Imitative play.
Games.

In studying his class, whether as individuals or as a group, the teacher may well use such a list as a basis for checking and recording his observations.

Constant observation, which may require a great deal of time, is necessary in order to learn the peculiar interests of the individuals in a given group. Many good teachers make a list or inventory of the interests of the various members of the class as they observe them. These lists constitute a valuable source of reference when they make plans for the lesson period. Since these interests are being constantly modified by conditions in the environment of each pupil, the teacher must be constantly revising his inventories and reshaping his plans. Some event of current interest in the community, some unusual happening in the family, some impending event—these and many similar incidents are constantly stimulating intense interest. The wise teacher, alert to such conditions, will seize upon them to develop worthy purposes on the part of the members of his class and to provide such activities as will result in the pupils learning what he wants them to learn.

This use of interest requires that the teacher's plans be flexible. They cannot be set out completely in advance and then rigidly followed. Suppose for example, one tries to teach a prescribed lesson to a group of Junior boys who only the day before attended a circus. Imagine his trying to teach a lesson, however important, that could in no way utilize the interest that is still alive and flaming from the experiences of the preceding day. The boys will want to talk about the circus. They will probably do so whether the teacher wills it or not. Why not plan wisely to lead the spirited discussion so that some important objective may be achieved?

With older learners immediate interests are of less consequence although they are still the necessary basis of teaching. Mature learners, because of their interest in biblical truth, may have their attention called to the teaching of a selected passage of Scripture and may purposefully seek to learn the facts about it and the truth contained in it. Even so, the teacher must so guide the discussion that it will have a point of definite interest for the members of the class.

The lesson helps furnished to teachers supply many valuable suggestions for relating the lesson material to the several interests of various age groups. When a teacher begins to plan for a class period, therefore, he may do well to study his lesson helps to find some suggested approach to his class on the basis of the interests which he thinks they already have.

VI. ATTENTION INDICATES INTEREST

How may teachers know that their pupils are genuinely interested in what is going on in the classroom? Any clever teacher can secure attention for the moment. Even an unskilled teacher can secure some activity of pupils who have no particular interest in the thing they are doing. Sustained interest and attention to an enterprise, however, depend upon the active interest of the learners in the matter under consideration. If their attention is scattered or fleeting, the teacher may know that he has failed to find a point of common interest vitally related to what he is trying to do. On the other hand, their sustained attention is due to an interest that he may use for developing an active purpose. Effective teaching depends upon the agreement of learner and teacher in a common worthy purpose.

VII. SUSTAINING INTEREST

Teachers often assume that they can stimulate an active interest after the class has assembled on Sunday morning, develop the essential facts and truths in the proposed lesson, and then dismiss the whole affair until the following Sunday, at which time another series of interests will be treated in a similar manner. However, interest sufficiently strong to stimulate purposeful activity toward desired learning does not develop so rapidly, nor can it be dismissed so easily. Interest and purpose must continue through the week, and from Sunday to Sunday.

Many of the lesson helps take into consideration the necessity of such continuity although sometimes the suggested lesson outlines shift abruptly from one Sunday to the next. The difficulty at this point is not so great in the teaching of adults as it is with children. Care should be taken to test a series of lessons for a thread of possible interest to the group. If it is not easily found, the teacher should endeavor to make such additions and adaptations as he may think necessary to secure the desired thread of interest.

VIII. THE TEACHER A FACTOR IN SECURING INTEREST

The teacher himself is frequently a deciding factor in arousing interest and securing attention. He may easily secure the interest of the class in that in which he himself is interested. His own attitudes, appreciations, habits and skills are vital factors in arousing the interest of his pupils and challenging their attention. He may have more or less of that indefinable trait which we call originality. If more, fine; if less, he may do much to atone for its lack. Some elements in personality are born in us; if they are totally lacking, we cannot develop them. Other elements we may acquire; and still others, present in small degree, we may cultivate to a high degree.

IX. SIGNIFICANCE OF THIS DISCUSSION

We have seen that learning is an active process, depending on purpose. Purpose comes from interest; and interest, which is largely determined by needs, is the key to attention. If a teacher wishes to have the attention of his class, he must lead his pupils to realize their needs, and to see that by studying the subject matter and participating in the class activities, they can at least partially meet their needs. This sense of need, accompanied by the feeling that the need can be met by participating in the class activities, will arouse and sustain their interest; and this awakened and sustained interest will guarantee their attention. If the teacher really knows the needs of his pupils, both collectively and individually, and if he is master of his subject matter, familiar with teaching principles, and skilled in teaching methods, he may expect that the interest and attention of his pupils will largely take care of themselves. He will have no need to resort to artifical and extraneous methods to secure attendance and attention.

Too often teachers approach attention from the wrong end, and thereby defeat their efforts to teach creatively. Knowing that they must have it if they are to help their pupils, they make securing attention a direct aim and think of devices by which they may secure it. They should approach it indirectly, by thinking of the pupils' needs and of how to get them to realize these needs. To the extent that teachers succeed in doing this, they will secure the vital interest of the pupils in the class activities and in the subject matter necessary to carry on these activities. Pupils will study, be present on time, anxious to participate, alert, teachable, resentful of intrusion or of anything that interferes with the teacher's efforts to help them.

Of course this kind of teaching requires time and effort. It means reading and study, and attending teachers' meetings, both in the church and at various denominational gatherings. It calls for vision, consecration, energy, purpose, stedfastness. It cannot be fully achieved in a five-night study course, however much such a course may help. Difficulties must be surmounted; handicaps must be overcome. The Sunday school teacher encounters difficulties that the public school teacher does not have to face. The attendance of his pupils is voluntary and recitations are a week apart; subject matter is not so abundant, and often it may not seem so directly vital to pupil needs; and limits of time and often of equipment are serious handicaps.

To whatever extent we may help our learners in their development of a Christlike personality, we must do it week by week, much of it through our use of the lesson material in the classroom. If we are to command their attention through an aroused interest because of a realization of specific needs, we must study faithfully and prepare thoroughly week by week. However familiar we may be with subject matter, we must study it anew properly to master and use it; we must carefully plan how we will teach; we must go to our classes ready and eager, expectant and prayerful, conscious of God's presence and endued with his Spirit. Only so may we awaken in our pupils a sense of need, and thereby arouse interest, inspire purpose, and secure attention.

TEACHING SUGGESTIONS

Questions for Study and Review

1. What means are usually suggested for holding attention?
2. Show that teaching is not so simple a process as this would indicate.
3. Discuss the statement, "Learning is an active process."
4. What is the relation of "worthy purposes" to interest?
5. What of "utilizing interests"?
6. What of arousing mental attitudes?
7. What is your idea of the value of cataloging interests?
8. State the necessity for flexible plans.
9. "Attention indicates interest." What is the significance of this for the teacher?
10. Discuss "sustaining interest."
11. Show the significance of this whole discussion to the teacher.
12. Tell of the teacher as a factor in securing interest.

Topical Outline

Attention Really a Profound Necessity

I. LEARNING AN ACTIVE PROCESS
II. DEVELOPING WORTHY PURPOSES
III. UTILIZING INTERESTS
IV. AROUSING MENTAL ATTITUDES
V. CATALOGING INTERESTS
VI. ATTENTION INDICATES INTEREST
VII. SUSTAINING INTEREST
VIII. THE TEACHER A FACTOR IN SECURING INTEREST
IX. SIGNIFICANCE OF THIS DISCUSSION

VII

TEACHERS SHOULD PROVIDE SUITABLE
LEARNING ACTIVITIES

Growth in the direction indicated by his objectives whether in knowledge or conduct will not necessarily take place simply because teacher and learner are engaged in activity. The activities must have meaning and purpose. The meaning and purpose must be clear and unmistakable both for the teacher and the learner. It is the duty of the teacher to see that the purposes are clear, that the meaning of the activities engaged in and the subject matter utilized are properly understood. Careful thought and inquiry on the part of the teacher may be required in order to assure this desired understanding.

The teacher may be tempted to assume that his learners have a clear understanding of the purpose of their study and activities because they follow through certain assignments. Experience shows that engaging in an effort or activity even for a long time does not necessarily indicate a clear understanding of the deeper meanings involved. The reader may be familiar with the story of the old car-wheel knocker at the railway station. At the age of seventy he was retired and a banquet was given in honor of his long and faithful service. The superintendent acted as toastmaster and was eloquent in his praise of the most faithful employee whose careful, intelligent work through the years had meant safety to thousands of passengers. After the eulogy the superintendent asked the retired man if he had anything to say. "Yes," said he, "I have always been curious about one thing; something that I have never been able to understand." "Then go right ahead," replied the superintendent; "if we can supply the information we shall be glad to do so."

"Well, then," said the old man, "I have been curious for nigh onto forty years to know just why you had me knockin' on them car wheels every time the train came in."

It is likewise a mistake too often made to assume because a subject or purpose is clearly understood by the teacher that it is therefore simple enough for the pupil to understand it. The maturity of the learner, his previous experience and training, must be carefully taken into account.

The mental and spiritual state and progress of the learner must be constantly considered. This statement is perfectly obvious and will meet with instant acceptance. Its implications and bearings, however, are neither so simple nor so obvious. So far-reaching and vital are these implications that they must underlie all efforts to teach.

For example, the logical organization of facts and subject matter may be well suited to the adult mind which is measurably trained to think consecutively and to see things as a whole. Such logical organization, however, has little significance for children. This may account for the fact that teachers who are accustomed to teach adults find it difficult to guide the learning activities of children. This also makes necessary special lessons and special lesson treatments for children such as are provided in the Graded Lesson Series.

Thus the manner and order in which materials are presented should be determined by the way in which the learner learns most readily and effectively, and not necessarily by the way in which the teacher would arrange them for his own use. This makes it necessary that many materials and ideas in connection with a given lesson, even though they are important, be omitted for the time, and treatment of them postponed until the learner is more mature. Jesus recognized this principle when he said to his disciples, "I have yet many things to say unto you, but ye cannot bear them now" (John 16:12).

There are many kinds of learning activities which the teacher is called upon to direct. A complete classification of these could hardly be made, but for our present purpose the following general classification may be helpful.

Learning activities which develop the ability to do; specific habits and skills.

Learning activities which develop understanding. This marks an upward step.

Learning activities which develop a sense of worth and value; attitudes and appreciations.

It should be obvious to the teacher that the third aspect of the learning process mentioned necessarily involves the other two. However, for convenience they are treated separately. We now consider some things which the teacher may do in directing each of these types of learning.

Ability to Do

While we look to our public schools to develop most of the specific abilities that have to do with learning, the Sunday school teacher should be ready at all times to assist his learners in acquiring or improving various skills. Moreover, some skills are of special use in the Sunday school. Foremost among these is facility in the use of the Bible. Early in the life of the pupil he should learn to use the Bible as his chief source of religious information and inspiration. He should be encouraged to practice making references to it. He should become so familiar with it that he can use it quickly and accurately. And, although the teacher should not set out to develop and perfect this skill before engaging in other learning activities or before the learner has developed a conscious need for the ability to use the Bible, he should give much attention to it as need arises. In addition to merely practicing the use of the Bible for reference as need arises for it, frequent opportunity should be provided for special drills that will develop both speed and accuracy. As a rule, this may be effectively done with Juniors and Intermediates. However, if older pupils show inability to use the Bible, the teacher should tactfully secure practice until they acquire the necessary skill.

As is well known, a concordance offers in alphabetical order certain key words occuring in Scripture passages together with references showing where these passages may be found. When the pupil wishes to find a given passage, he recalls some word in that passage, looks up that word in his concordance and thus finds where the passage is to be found in the Bible. There is a limited concordance in every Teacher's Bible; a more extended concordance may be purchased for a reasonable sum. Leaders of teacher training groups and all teachers from the Junior department up should see to it that their pupils understand fully and clearly the proper uses of a concordance.

Similar to the concordance, and also furnished in the Teacher's Bible, is the subject index. This the pupil may use to locate apt scripture references to a given subject. The subjects are listed in the subject index in alphabetical order. The pupil will turn to the particular subject in which he is interested and there find the Scripture passages which mention that subject. One can hardly study the Bible intelligently who has not acquired skill in using the concordance and the subject index.

Likewise, all teachers of the Bible should use maps and devlop in their learners skill in using maps. How can the life and travels of Abraham or Moses or Paul, for example, be clearly grasped without the use of maps? It is not sufficient for the teacher himself to use maps; it is equally important that he develop in his pupils habits and skills in their use.

General reference works are also necessary for intelligent Bible study, both on the part of the teacher and the learner. A book or a series of books treating Bible history may be helpful for general Bible study and for the study and teaching of particular lessons as well. Biographies of Bible characters, such as Abraham, Moses,

Joshua, Samuel, David, and other Old Testament heroes, along with the life of Christ, and lives of Paul and other New Testament leaders, should be regarded as indispensable.

The skills here presented are merely suggestive. The teacher should discover the needs of his pupils with respect to any specific ability and then set about providing activities that will help them to develop and improve the needed ability. Once the reason for developing a given skill is clear to the learner, he will engage in drills and practice to perfect it.

Understanding

If our teaching is to be effective in developing Christian conduct, the learner must be led into understanding. Long ago, a Christian teacher asked a certain eager inquirer, "Understandest thou what thou readest?" This is always a proper question for those who essay to teach the Scriptures. We are to lead our pupils to an understanding of what is read, of what is said, of the deeper things of the Holy Writings.

Because these deeper things are often more or less difficult and complex, a variety of activities may be necessary before a given understanding is fully developed. Too often the teacher relies on a single definition or statement or experience, only to find that the learner's understanding is distorted or incomplete. Often the learner, too timid to ask for explanations, fails to get an adequate idea of the thing to be understood. In the old rhyme about the six blind men who went to "see" the elephant, each, through the sense of touch, obtained what he thought was an adequate understanding of the nature of the elephant. However, the rhyme ends with—

> And so these men of Indostan
>   Disputed loud and long,
> Each in his own opinion
>   Exceeding stiff and strong,
> Though each was partly in the right,
>   And all were in the wrong.

Many types of activities are required in order to develop understandings or generalizations. Furthermore, each new experience tends to modify the understanding previously held. A county superintendent and his friend visited a rural school for Indians. During the course of the visit the teacher called the children to order and introduced the visitors. He introduced the friend as Doctor X—. At once a little Indian began to scream hysterically. Investigation revealed that shortly before this time the county health officer had come to the school and vaccinated all the children. The little Indian heard the teacher address the visitor as "Doctor." To him a "doctor" was some one who does painful things to the arm. Now, however, he had reason to modify his previous generalization which, no doubt, could he have stated it, would have been, "Doctors are men that hurt children's arms."

Types of learning activities most commonly used to develop understanding may be designated as object teaching, use of pictures, lecture, discussion, debate, dramatization, reading, problem solving, and various types of creative expression. Most of these represent activities that may easily be used by the Sunday school teacher. In planning activities for developing understanding, he should exercise care to see that the selected activity is not too complicated for the learner to engage in successfully. Simplicity and directness should be the constant aim of the teacher.

The teacher should plan the activity so that it will involve a number of elements with which the learner is already familiar. "What is it like?" is about the first question one asks when brought to consider some new thing or idea involving understanding. "What is it for?" "where did it come from?" and "how does it work?" are questions that indicate the necessity of providing familiar elements in a new learning situation. The Master Teacher recognized the need of utilizing familiar situations in developing understanding of the important truths he wished to teach. Thus he made frequent use of the parable. "The kingdom of heaven," said he, "is as a man traveling into a far country. . . ." Peter asked him, "How oft shall my brother sin against me and I forgive him?" Jesus answered, "Until seventy times seven." And then to develop a proper understanding of the real meaning of forgiveness, he said, "Therefore is the kingdom of heaven likened unto a certain king, which would take account of his servants. . ." (Matthew 18:23-35).

In selecting readings to develop understanding, the teacher should exercise care regarding language difficulty. In many instances it is assumed that language will be intelligible to the learner because it appears simple enough to the teacher. As a rule he cannot rely upon the pupil to stop and make inquiry regarding the meaning of words. The pupil's tendency is rather to skip the "hard words" and be content with a hazy idea of what he reads. Fortunately, many reading lists, with suggestions as to types of readers for which they are appropriate, are now available.

The purpose of a learning activity should be clear both to teacher and learner. When needed, specific directions should be provided by the teacher. If reading is suggested, then it should be made clear to the learner just why the particular story or scripture passage is being read. If a discussion is engaged in, the purpose, the main point, should be kept clearly in the foreground at all times. Many a spirited discussion has been practically useless as a learning activity simply because it was permitted to drift aimlessly in whatever direction some whim dictated.

Ample opportunity should be provided for the learner to use his own initiative. Self-expression should be encouraged through any medium the learner may desire to use. Many a pupil does not have the ability to express himself freely in speech or in writing, but this does not mean necessarily that he has not developed understandings. Perhaps he has some other form of expression that should be encouraged. Can he paint or draw? Can he write a poem? Can he collect rare specimens of some sort? Can he participate in a dramatic production? Whatever means may be at hand whereby the learner may give expression to his understanding of the truth to be learned, the teacher should recognize and encourage.

Attitudes

The development of proper attitudes is the height of good teaching. This requires activities of all the types previously mentioned. It involves purposeful activities in which the learner will have opportunity to react to situations in which the desired attitude is a factor. Talking about attitudes is often helpful. Reading about people who have exhibited desirable attitudes in situations that may easily be interpreted is stimulating. However, the individual does not really acquire or develop an attitude unless he is given opportunity to express it.

In a certain school great stress was laid upon training the pupils in the "worthy use of leisure." Teachers talked about it. The principal emphasized it. Parents became enthusiastic. Pupils anticipated joyfully the opportunity to do all the wonderful things they could imagine as worthy use of their leisure time. But the pupils failed to develop sound judgments or proper habits in the use of their leisure time. What was the trouble? The reason was not difficult to find. Not a single period of the school day was set aside during which the pupils were free to do as they would. They could not learn how to use leisure time because they were given no leisure time to use.

And so it is with all Christian attitudes which the Sunday school teacher seeks to engender. Would he have his pupils take a sympathetic attitude toward those in distress? Let him lead them to face a situation in which distress is present, and where they have opportunity to do something about it. Would he have them learn to cooperate with others? Then let him provide, or utilize, some opportunity for them to work together in a common enterprise. Would he teach them reverence? Then let him provide opportunities for them to experience situations in which reverence is manifest.

Often teachers become so greatly interested in teaching details that the attitudes which motivate conduct are overlooked. Jesus had something like this in mind when he reprimanded the scribes and Pharisees with one of the severest utterances that ever fell from his lips: "Woe unto you, scribes and Pharisees, hypocrites! for ye pay tithe of mint and anise and cummin, and have omitted the weightier matters of the law, judgment, mercy, and faith; these ought ye to have done, and not to leave the other undone" (Matthew 23:23).

Activities should be progressive. As the learner grows, the learning activities should become more complex and varied. To engage in the same activities in the same way Sunday after Sunday soon becomes tiresome and ineffective, but this practice characterizes a multitude of Sunday schools. The familiar Friday afternoon scene in the rural school of a generation ago brings this fact forcibly to mind. It was generally the custom to devote Friday afternoon to reciting poems, essays, or orations that had been memorized for the occasion. The practice afforded both recreation and the opportunity to develop the art of public speaking. Many a forceful public speaker attributes his success to the "speech making" in which he engaged on those Friday afternoons. In most of these rural schools the pupils were glad to learn new "speeches" from time to time, and thus enrich their store of literature and enlarge their power of expression. In every school, however, there was usually some boy who memorized a single stanza or brief poem. Week after week, after the other pupils recited their "new speeches," he came forward and repeated the same selection in much the same way. Because he engaged in no new activity no growth took place, no learning was accomplished.

Activities, if they are to result in learning, must lead to added interest and additional effort on the part of the learner. In other words, they must be progressive. To plan and guide such progressive activities constitutes the heart of the teacher's work.

TEACHING SUGGESTIONS

Questions for Study and Review

1. Show that activities must have meaning and purpose.
2. What are some mistakes commonly made by teachers as regards learning activities?
3. Explain why a logical organization of material may not be the best presentation.
4. Indicate the three types of learning activities discussed in this chapter.
5. What are some specific abilities which should be acquired in the Sunday school?
6. Show how a variety of activities is necessary in order to develop understandings. What types of activities are suggested for this purpose?
7. How did the Master Teacher develop understandings?
8. Can attitudes be developed wholly apart from conduct? What does this suggest as to suitable learning activities for developing desirable attitudes?
9. Illustrate how teaching detailed facts may prevent our achieving the larger objectives of our teaching.

Topical Outline

OBSERVATIONS ABOUT LEARNING ACTIVITIES

I. ABILITY TO DO
  1. The Sunday school should develop certain skills
  2. Particularly in the use of the Bible

II. UNDERSTANDING
  1. "Understandest thou what thou readest?"
  2. Variety of activities necessary
  3. Should involve familiar elements
  4. Should provide initiative for learner

III. ATTITUDES
  1. The height of good teaching
  2. Exercise must be provided
  3. Activities should be progressive

VIII

TEACHERS SHOULD PLAN THEIR TEACHING

Anything worth doing is worthy of careful planning. Certainly, anything as important and complicated as teaching a Sunday school lesson should be attempted only with careful consideration of every phase of the undertaking. Too often a teacher attempts to conduct the work of a class when it is evident that he has thought out no particular plan for doing it. The results of such procedure are discouraging and may be positively harmful. Planning in advance is necessary even though, when the time for teaching arrives, the plans may have to be modified. In fact, an important part of the teacher's planning should include such contingencies.

Thus far the various important elements that enter into the teaching-learning process have been considered separately. However, the successful work of the teacher requires that for each lesson period he make plans for each of these elements to function in proper relation to all the others. The truths to be taught, as indicated in the objectives, the nature and the interests of the learner, the learning activities to be engaged in, the materials and subject matter to be used, the procedures to be followed, and the means of testing or evaluating the results of the teaching—all of these must be carefully considered in advance and a plan of action developed. It is not possible or desirable to set forth explicitly in this book a plan for the teacher to follow in every detail. However, certain general suggestions are made for the guidance of teachers as they plan their work.

I. Begin Early

Careful teachers begin the study of a new lesson as soon as possible after an old lesson has been taught.

Sunday afternoon is an excellent and, with many, a favored time to begin the preparation of the next lesson. The time element here, as elsewhere, is important—time to pray, time to meditate, time to go down into the lesson, time to go afield to see what others have thought, time to make the truths of the lesson one's very own.

There is a deeper reason for beginning early than may at first appear. If during Sunday afternoon or evening we make our first study of the Scripture passage which we are to teach the following Sunday, we have the week in which to study and meditate upon it. We may think upon it as we go about our daily duties, as we walk back and forth to business, as we ride the street cars, as we engage in our accustomed tasks in the home or business. We may, as occasion arises, discuss it with other teachers, with the pastor, or with other Bible scholars. Thus it will be possible to go to the class with a depth and fulness of understanding and with a richness of appreciation which might otherwise be unattainable.

II. BEGIN WITH THE BIBLE

Since the Bible furnishes the material for the Sunday school lesson, all planning may well begin with it. Whether the topics are outlined in the Uniform or the Graded Lessons, or in any other series, let us study thoroughly the proposed Scripture passage. Read the printed passage; read it repeatedly; read the larger lesson of which it is a part. With the help of a reference Bible and lesson helps, let us read other portions of Scripture that shed light on it. We should read it in the original if possible. We may read it at least in some other translation than the one ordinarily used. We should do original thinking and gather treasures directly from the Book. Such first-hand, direct study of the Bible will greatly reward us.

III. LIST AIMS OR OBJECTIVES

Having made the truth of the Scripture passages our own, next let us list some objectives or aims that will guide us in our teaching. As a rule, the lesson helps suggest desirable objectives. However, after having become thoroughly familiar with the truths in the proposed lesson, we should ask ourselves a number of questions and write out the answers. What truths suggested in the Bible passage involve skills, understandings, attitudes that may profitably become the basis of class activities? What experiences have the learners had that will provide a basis for purposeful activity? What learning activities may be suggested? Do the interests that we have discovered among our learners suggest the possibility of developing a purpose around which to organize suitable learning activities? Which activities suggest themselves as proper for beginning, which for developing, and which for closing, the lesson period?

IV. RESTUDY PUPILS' INTERESTS AND NEEDS

It is not sufficient to study and catalog once for all the interests, the environmental conditions, and the needs of our individual pupils. Each lesson plan requires that we canvass carefully all available information that may help us to understand the circumstances that surround the class and that may affect the learning of each member. Any new or unusual happening, any condition that may have developed during the week, any manifestation of special interest during the previous class period, we should carefully note and keep in mind as we develop our plans for the next class period. To guard against leaving this to chance we should carefully write down all observations. We may well ask: What interest was developed during the last lesson period that may carry over to next Sunday? What unusual general event has occurred during the week that may be of especial interest to my learners? What individual experiences has some pupil had that may affect his interests?

V. RIGHTLY DIVIDE THE TIME

Having asked and answered such questions, we are now ready to list suggested activities in the order in which

the pupils may engage in them. The time of the lesson
period will probably not much exceed thirty minutes.
This time must be utilized to the fullest possible extent,
for it is a sacred trust, and every moment must be made
to count; not one must be lost. There must be no inter-
ruptions, and the lesson plan must be so flexible that it
can be adjusted to any needs that may develop.

It is of the utmost importance, as is elsewhere suggested, that the concluding moments of the class period
be without interruption or confusion. Often a splendid
beginning and the strong development of a lesson fail to
result in effective teaching because the teacher saves no
time for an orderly, forceful conclusion. Careful planning
in advance will go far toward avoiding such a situation
and provide for the orderly, unhurried development of
the lesson to its conclusion.

VI. Select Suitable Materials

The Bible is the primary source for subject matter,
but much valuable material from other sources may be
often utilized to good advantage. In order that we may
have adequate materials at hand when needed, it is well
to make a list of all available materials for effective use
in the proposed learning activities. Types of materials
frequently used are here suggested.

Objects. A direct and effective means of understanding is through the use of objects. To see a thing, handle
it, taste it, smell it, ask questions about its use, and
compare it with other things with which we are familiar,
constitutes one of the principal means of learning. There
are limits, of course, to the use of this kind of teaching
material. Perhaps the object about which the teacher
desires to develop understanding is not available. Possibly it is to be found only in some foreign country. In
this case, other means must be provided. However, many
objects useful in teaching are to be found on every hand.
They are all about us. Their very abundance and acces-
sibility often result in our failure to appreciate and use
them. We should be constantly on the alert for objects

that may be utilized in teaching. We may find a fruitful source of interesting objects helpful in Bible teaching in the homes of people in the community who, having had the advantages of foreign travel, have brought back interesting things from other lands. Usually they are glad to make their treasures available. Frequently, they will visit the class and discuss various objects and their experiences with them.

Pictures. When we cannot bring to the classroom the various objects about which we desire to develop understandings, we may bring pictures as a good substitute. Inexpensive pictures of almost anything are now easily obtainable. As with objects, so with pictures; frequently they are right at hand in abundance. Pupils can easily be interested in locating and procuring a wide variety of them. Next to seeing the object itself, a good picture may be the best way to gain an understanding of it. We may well make a list of pictures that are suggestive of good teaching materials, and add to it from time to time as other suitable pictures come to our attention. A cumulative list, or better still a card index of available pictures is of much help in planning suitable matter for use in connection with lesson plans.

Printed Materials. For classes whose members are old enough to read there is an increasing amount of printed material available for use in teaching. Stories, descriptive materials, travel books, and reference books of all kinds may be found in most communities. Even for remote rural communities, there are usually library facilities in some adjacent city or town where printed materials may be secured. The lesson helps prepared by the Sunday School Board are valuable, for they make available the resources of the libraries of those who devote their time to searching for suitable teaching materials, and suggest possible uses for them. Many good teachers keep extensive files or "scrap books" into which they put any printed material that they think may be useful as subject matter in their teaching.

Personal Experiences. Experience is the best teacher. Some even go so far as to say that it is the only teacher. Certainly there is no richer source of subject matter than that of experience. We teachers cannot pass on our experience to the learners, but they may vicariously experience much of what has touched and influenced us and others. Therefore, in planning our work we should look into our own experiences for those things that may be helpful to our learners in gaining the desired understandings. Many good teachers keep a careful diary from which they extract statements of experiences that will help them in their teaching.

Care should be exercised at this point, for pupils frequently become wearied when, lesson after lesson, their chief activity is that of listening to a recital of the teacher's experiences. If the teacher thinks of using his personal experiences as subject matter, he should be certain that it is the best means at hand for developing the desired understanding. Occasionally a teacher collects anecdotes from the experiences of others and relates them as if they were his own experiences. This should never be done. Not only is it dishonest, but it often smacks of an insincerity which the learner clearly perceives.

VII. OUTLINE DEFINITE PROCEDURES

With the objectives, suggested activities and materials in hand, the final phase of planning is that of stating probable procedures for introducing the lesson period, developing the lesson, and concluding it. The nature of the activities planned and of the materials to be used will determine in large measure the manner of general procedure. However, we should not leave procedures to chance. We should determine specifically just how we expect to begin the lesson period. Shall we ask a question? If so, of whom shall we ask it? What are the probable responses that we may expect? How shall we follow them up? How much time may we reasonably use for preliminaries?

Similarly, we should as definitely as possible plan for every step during the developing and the concluding periods of the class activities. We should include alternative suggestions for adapting the procedure to possible changes that may arise.

VIII. Revise the Lesson Plan

Having developed the lesson plan so as to include all essential elements, we should carefully revise and refine the whole before we use it. This planning and preparation should be done as early as possible to allow ample time for the plan to mature in our minds. From then until the lesson period, we should point our reading and thought to the successful working out of the plan. Thus prepared, we may approach the lesson period with the assurance that we will do our best teaching and may hope for the best results.

TEACHING SUGGESTIONS

Questions for Study and Review

1. Why should the teacher carefully prepare a lesson plan?
2. Discuss the suggestion that the lesson plan should include all phases of the teaching process.
3. Why should the teacher make an early beginning of his lesson preparation?
4. Discuss the suggestion that the teacher should begin his lesson preparation with a study of the Bible itself.
5. Why should the teacher in his preparation list aims or objectives?
6. Why should he at this time restudy the interests and needs of the pupils?
7. What is the significance of rightly dividing the time?
8. Discuss the selection of suitable materials.
9. What definite procedures should be outlined?
10. Why revise the lesson plan?

Topical Outline

I. Begin Early

II. Begin with the Bible

III. List Aims or Objectives

IV. Restudy Pupils' Interests and Needs

V. Rightly Divide the Time

VI. Select Suitable Materials
1. Objects
2. Pictures
3. Printed materials
4. Personal experiences

VII. Outline Definite Procedures

VIII. Revise the Lesson Plan

IX

TEACHERS SHOULD TEST THEIR TEACHING

A hunter went out to shoot some birds. Later, when asked if he killed any, he replied, "I do not know. I aimed and shot at seven, but I did not take the trouble to find out whether I killed any of them." No one would have any confidence in this man's ability as a hunter.

Many Sunday school teachers are like that hunter in that they aim, and shoot, but do not try to find out if they hit anything. They want to help their pupils learn; they plan to help them; they try to work their plans; but they stop there—they do not try to find out whether they have achieved their aims. The only way in which they can find out is to test their teaching, measure the results. Educators call measuring results "evaluating (fixing the value of) teaching."

Testing the results of the work engaged in by teacher and learner constitutes one of the most important phases of the teaching-learning process. This is no less true of the work done in the Sunday school than in any other school. However, examinations, tests, and other means of evaluation so commonly used in the public schools have been but little used in the Sunday school. As a rule, a few questions calling for a recital of lesson facts constitute the sole means of ascertaining the results of teaching. Even this form of testing is made less effective by slavishly following the questions printed in the lesson helps.

Many teachers would be surprised at finding, by any fair testing of their work, how little their pupils have learned as a result of their teaching. Yet, in the important enterprise of directing the growth of the members of his class, it is the obligation of the teacher to be constantly appraising by every possible means the work that is done in the light of the objectives that have been set forth.

In every walk of life we are constantly checking up on our positions, our condition, and our progress. The mariner regularly makes soundings to ascertain the depth of the waters in which he is sailing; he regularly checks his position by the stars; he observes and records carefully the condition of the weather; he studies the condition of his ship and crew and keeps a detailed log of his journey in order that he may arrive safely in the port which is the object of his journey. No less important is it for the Sunday school teacher to appraise his teaching at every step as he endeavors to guide his learners into the way of all truth.

I. PURPOSE OF EVALUATION

Evaluation of teaching, as seen in the various kinds of examinations and tests, often falls short of the real purpose to be achieved. Often the examinations are a dreaded ordeal which the learner is asked to undergo. Too often, as has already been indicated, they consist of asking pupils to reproduce or recite a number of isolated facts without reference to their larger relationships. Instead of helping teacher and learner the better to chart their course, examinations often result in added confusion and discouragement. A test that merely leaves learner and teacher conscious that the results are defective at certain points is of no value unless it stimulates further activity to improve the situation. Standards of achievement are often set up in the form of numerical grades which have little or no value so far as reaching the desired objectives of teaching are concerned. Such use of tests or other means of evaluation may not only be practically useless as a means of improving teaching but may be, and often is positively harmful. This is all quite as true of teaching books in the Training Course as of teaching the lessons in the Sunday school.

The real purpose of testing the results of teaching is to assist in achieving the desired objectives. Therefore, the means employed should be such as will reveal the extent to which the class activities have advanced the learners in the desired direction and will indicate possible ways of improving the work of both learner and teacher. The teacher, having engaged in the work of the class period for achieving definite skills, understandings and attitudes, should carefully observe the outcomes of the process and interpret them in terms of his objectives. Has the desired skill been developed, the desired understanding been enriched and matured, the desired attitude been manifested in daily conduct?

II. EVALUATION A CONTINUOUS PROCESS

Viewed in this light, the evaluation of the results of teaching is not confined to an examination or test at the close of a week, or a month, or a year, to discover how much of the factual matter presented in the class can be remembered and reproduced by the learners. It is, rather, a continuous process in which both teacher and learner participate, and it includes those periods when special attention and emphasis are given to the evaluation of a given unit or of the whole course of study. At the end of a series of lessons devoted to the same general problem, opportunity should be provided to review or "new-view" the series. In this manner important relationships can be established which might not otherwise be possible.

Each lesson has its own truths which ought to be looked at in perspective at the lesson's close. Indeed, in their entirety and unity they cannot be looked at before. Reviewing a lesson to see it in perspective is quite different from reviewing it to discover the learner's understanding of it, or to test his knowledge of it, or to repeat it for the purpose of fixing it in his mind. However, as teacher and learner proceed in a series of learning activities the perspective constantly changes, and consequently they do not have to wait for some particular time or place to evaluate the work that has been done.

III. Pupil Evaluation

When the interests of the learner are so enlisted that he engages in purposeful activities, he will constantly judge his work to determine whether his activities are contributing to the achievement of his purpose. The forming of such judgments is in itself an important part of the educative process and should therefore receive the constant attention of the teacher. Throughout his life the learner will be engaged in forming judgments regarding his own activities. Practice in doing so under the wise guidance of the teacher is therefore of primary importance.

Since the final purpose of Sunday school teaching is to modify conduct to make it conform to Christian principles, evaluation of the results of teaching is of much greater significance than merely finding out how much the learner knows. The extent to which he learns to formulate his judgments and to modify his conduct accordingly is, indeed, the true test of teaching.

IV. Teacher Evaluation

Since the teacher is responsible for guiding learners in all of their learning activities, he should evaluate not only the work of the learner but also his own teaching as the results are revealed in the progress of the learners. Have his activities in planning and directing the work of the learners been as effective as he had anticipated? Were some of his activities untimely or inappropriate? Were there other procedures that might have been more effective? Such stock-taking should engage his earnest attention after each teaching effort, and the results should be used in planning the work for the next class period.

Teacher evaluation includes not only self-evaluation but also careful observation of the results of the activities of each member of the class. Just as the activities of the learners have been suggested under three main divisions, so the teacher's activities in evaluating the work of the class may well be considered under these same divisions.

1. *Specific Habits and Skills.* Having set up certain desirable habits which he wishes his learners to develop, the teacher should discover means of determining how well these habits are being developed. This type of evaluation lends itself readily to the use of questions and drill exercises. The exactness with which questions are answered, and the speed and accuracy of performing specific skills may be observed and the difficulties noted. The results will suggest such additional activities as may be helpful for further developing desired skill.

Numerous objective or "new type" tests have been devised during recent years for use in the public schools. Such tests have many advantages when properly used. They may be made very interesting to the pupil, and the results are easily checked and scored. In fact, the pupil may often participate in making and in scoring them.

An objective test for biblical knowledge has been developed in two distinct parts. One part is to be given the pupils at a lesson period near the beginning of a Sunday school year (October), and the other eleven months later. No question in the second test appears in the first test, but the two tests are of the same difficulty. By grading or scoring the pupils on the first test and recording the results, and then doing the same with the second test, any improvement in the grade or score of a pupil will indicate his growth in biblical knowledge during the year.

2. *Understandings.* Here again questions are very useful in evaluating the work of the learner. However, questions for this purpose must be essentially different from those which merely test the retention of facts. "Thought questions" should be developed to secure responses which will indicate whether or not the learner has developed the desired understanding. In addition

to questions, means should be provided for the learner to use his understanding in a meaningful situation. If observation shows that the learner's understanding is hazy and uncertain, the teacher should devise additional means for making the meaning clear.

3. *Attitudes.* Just as the provision of means for developing desirable attitudes is a most difficult phase of the teaching process, so providing the means of determining whether the desired attitudes have been developed is the most difficult phase of evaluation. Too often the teacher assumes that evidence of the development of habits, skills, and understandings is sufficient warrant that the desired attitudes have been secured. This by no means follows. Many a person who can repeat promptly and accurately the essential facts of the Scriptures and give evidence that he has grasped the generalizations involved still lacks the proper attitudes for assuring Christian conduct.

Asking the learner to state his attitude with respect to a given situation may be helpful, but it is not a sufficient means for determining just what the attitude is.

The Master Teacher recognized this fact and gave us clear and unmistakable teaching concerning it:—

> Beware of false prophets, which come to you in sheep's clothing, but inwardly they are ravening wolves. Ye shall know them by their fruits.

> Not every one that saith unto me, Lord, Lord, shall enter into the kingdom of heaven; but he that doeth the will of my Father which is in heaven.

The proper test regarding an attitude, then, is how the individual acts when confronted with a situation in which the attitude is a factor. It becomes the task of the teacher to observe the conduct of his learner in life situations. Is the learner reverent? It is important that he know the meaning of reverence; that he can define it and cite examples of it. The real test however is, how does he behave in the house of the Lord? What does he do when God's people are at worship? Is he habitually in a reverent attitude when prayer is being offered? Granting that the teacher may mistake discreet silence for reverence, careful observation from time to time enforced by observations regarding other kindred attitudes will make it possible for the teacher to form a very good estimate of the extent to which the learner has acquired the desired attitude.

In recent years numerous attempts have been made to develop standardized tests of attitudes. Some of these tests are rather widely used in the public schools. Many of them are helpful and may well be studied by the Sunday school teacher. Among these are tests that deal with moral or ethical problems and are called "ethical discrimination tests." Those that reveal what the pupils think about religious teachings and doctrines are called "religious thinking tests." There are also behavior or conduct tests which give a clue to the kind of behavior pupils will manifest in various situations. After all, however, the careful observations of a prayerful teacher are about as reliable as any means yet developed.

V. The Final Test of Teaching

Whatever detailed evidences we may have of successful teaching the final test is to be found in the lives of those whom we teach. Have our learners discovered the truth of God as it is in Christ Jesus? Have they come to a saving knowledge of him? Have they accepted him as their personal Saviour and acknowledged him as Lord? Have they followed him in baptism? Are they engaged in Christlike service to their fellowmen? Are they using their God-given talents for his glory? Are they supporting his cause with their goods and their services? Are they publishing the Good News even to the uttermost parts of the earth? Are they living Christlike lives in every area of life? These are the test questions which determine in the end the effectiveness of our teaching. The extent to which evidences of these Christian virtues are not observable in the lives of our learners marks the extent to which our teaching is defective.

God has a mysterious way of bringing his will to pass. We cannot always see the evidences of the results of our teaching. Only he can know the final outcome of our efforts to teach. The consecrated Christian teacher who gives his best to his teaching in the fear of the Lord, even though because of human limitations he cannot answer with certainty these all-important questions, may have the assurance:

So shall my word be that goeth forth out of my mouth: it shall not return unto me void, but it shall accomplish that which I please, and it shall prosper in the thing whereto I sent it (Isa. 55:11).

TEACHING SUGGESTIONS
Questions for Study and Review

1. What is the usual practice as regards tests in the Sunday school with which you are associated?
2. In the light of the teaching in this chapter what tests do you think would be practicable and possible in your school?
3. State precisely the purpose of evaluation (1) negatively, (2) positively.
4. In what sense is evaluation to be a continuous process?
5. What of pupil evaluation?
6. Discuss teacher evaluation.
7. State with brief discussion some lines along which the teacher may test his teaching.
8. What is the final test of teaching?

Topical Outline
NECESSITY OF TESTS

I. PURPOSE OF EVALUATION

II. EVALUATION A CONTINUOUS PROCESS

III. PUPIL EVALUATION

IV. TEACHER EVALUATION
    1. Habits and skills
    2. Understandings
    3. Attitudes

V. THE FINAL TEST OF TEACHING

DIRECTIONS FOR THE TEACHING AND STUDY OF THIS BOOK FOR CREDIT

I. Directions for the Teacher

1. Ten class periods of forty-five minutes each, or the equivalent, are required for the completion of a book for credit.

2. The teacher should request an award on the book taught.

3. The teacher shall give a written examination covering the subject matter in the textbook. The examination may take the form of assigned work to be done between the class sessions, in the class sessions, or as a final examination.

Exception: All who attend all of the class sessions; who read the book through by the close of the course; and who, in the judgment of the teacher, do the classwork satisfactorily may be exempted from taking the examination.

4. Application for Sunday school awards should be sent to the state Sunday school department on proper application forms. These forms should be made in triplicate. Keep the last copy for the church file, and send the other two copies.

II. Directions for the Student *

1. *In Classwork*

(1) The student must attend at least six of the ten forty-five minute class periods to be entitled to take the class examination.

(2) The student must certify that the textbook has been read. (In rare cases where students may find it impracticable to read the book before the completion of the classwork, the teacher may accept a promise to read the book carefully within the next two weeks. This applies only to students who do the written work.)

(3) The student must take a written examination, making a minimum grade of 70 per cent, or qualify according to *Exception* noted above.

2. *In Individual Study by Correspondence*

Those who for any reason wish to study the book without the guidance of a teacher will use one of the following methods:

(1) Write answers to the questions printed in the book, or

(2) Write a summary of each chapter or a development of the chapter outlines.

In either case the student must read the book through.

Students may find profit in studying the text together, but where awards are requested, individual papers are required. Carbon copies or duplicates in any form cannot be accepted.

All written work done by such students on books for Sunday school credit should be sent to the state Sunday school secretary.

III. This Book Gives Credit in Section III of the Sunday School Training Course.

(* *The student must be fifteen years of age or older to receive Sunday school credit.*)